The
Music
Of

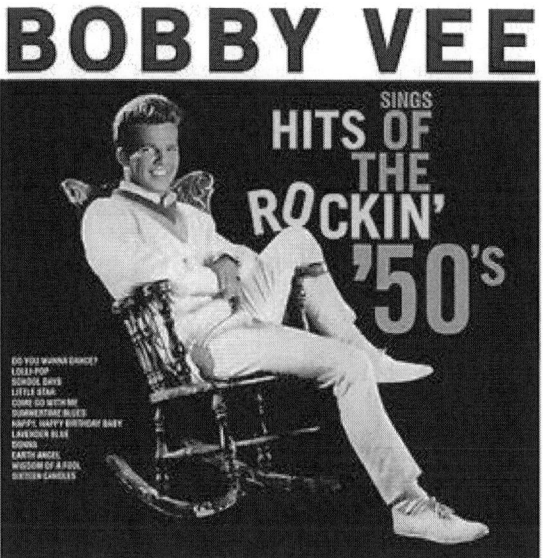

Robert Reynolds

Books by Robert Reynolds:

Firing at Shadows
A Perilous Place
Settler
East of Nowhere
Sentinels in the Sun
Monkeys in the Sun
Thunder Bay
Sorrowful
Trouble's Garden
Along the Quay
Showers In the Rain
A Fine Gray Rain
The Music of Bobby Vee
The Music of Hamilton, Joe Frank & Reynolds
The Music of Johnny Rivers

Due Out Soon:

Gray Wolf Pass

Contents

	Page
INTRODUCTION	**1**

PART ONE

1 HOLLY ON the RISE	**7**
2 VELLINE	**11**
3 A COLD WINTER	**21**
4 A FRIGID TOUR	**25**
5 AN UNFORSEEN BEGINNING	**31**
6 1960-62	**45**
7 1963-64	**59**
8 A REKINDLED CAREER	**73**
9 STELLAR CAREER WINDS DOWN	**87**

PART TWO

10 ALBUMS	**93**
11 SINGLES	**113**
12 MISCELLANEOUS MUSINGS	**117**
13 OVERSEAS	**129**

PART THREE

14 RECOGNITION and ACCOLADES	**133**

Robert Reynolds

The
Music
of
BOBBY VEE

INTRODUCTION

Robert Thomas Velline is one of the most consistent pop hit makers of the sixties, racking up 38 Top 100 hits between 1959-70. The handsome young man who would become famous as Bobby Vee scored hits of #1, #2, two at #3, two at #6 and several more in the Top Twenty. A vast number of his records resulted in two-sided hits, with both sides garnering significant airplay and generating sales.

The young man from Fargo, North Dakota also found success in several overseas markets, even reaching #2 on Great Britain's album chart in 1963.

During a period when flash-in-the-pan, one-hit-wonder teen idols often ruled the charts, Bobby Vee was a consistently reliable chart-topping singer. He was a talented musician who was as comfortable crooning a heart wrenching ballad, or belting out a bass-driven rocker, as he was singing a light and breezy teen ditty. But what few who did not follow his entire career realize is that many years after he had stopped being a significant force in the record industry, he made some of his best music.

Although this book is intended to provide insight into Bobby Vee's exceptional recording career, look briefly at his life, and examine his music, it is important to understand how his opportunity came about and how a then rising recording star named Buddy Holly affected his life. As the popular adage goes, "when one door closes, another one opens." This was especially true of the Bobby Vee/Buddy Holly connection.

Let us begin…

***

Artic winds howl off the Canadian plains—Saskatchewan, Manitoba—smack into America's heartland, bringing unexpected consequences for those inexperienced with the weather along the northern border. Winters are ruthless for those who are unaccustomed to the snow, the ice, the wicked winds and merciless subzero days and bitterly cold nights. Folks in the Dakotas plug what appear to be electrical umbilical cords into their parked vehicles to prevent them from freezing up. A good day in February is when the temperature creeps above zero.

Yes, it's that cold up there; it's that brutal. A traveler had better know what to expect when he sets out on a winter trek. The upper Midwest is no place to venture forth for the unprepared. Winters come early and stay long.

Folks across that part of the country are of robust stock; Northern European--Scandinavian. Germans. Swedes. Finns. They're folks who appreciate how unforgiving regional winters can be.

Winds whine. Temperatures plummet. Snow drifts. Down through the Dakotas, Nebraska, Kansas, Oklahoma the cruel winds blow relentlessly across treeless, rolling plains; for more than a thousand miles the terrain differs little from one end to the other. There is little to hinder the wind's treacherous advance once it begins.

As the crow flies, it's practically a straight shot from North Dakota's capital city of Fargo through the heart of the USA, all the way to the Texas Panhandle—Amarillo, Plainview, Levelland, Muleshoe, Buffalo Springs, Caprock, Floydada and Lubbock; twelve hundred miles across flatlands, rolling hills, barren wheat fields, and bleak grasslands.

Except for a geological oddity where the immense, winding Palo Duro Canyon carves a deep chasm across the plains thirty-miles south of Amarillo, there is little variation in the terrain along that entire length of mostly rich agricultural farmland where wheat, corn, sorghum, soybeans, and cotton grow.

With a little imagination, one might conclude that Fargo to the north and Lubbock to the south are identical twins—rural communities similar in size, agricultural makeup and relative isolation from the rest of the country—both being of ample distance to any major city or interstate thoroughfare. They are remote urban centers stuck pretty much in the middle of rural nowhere.

The two isolated towns even claim notorious residency in that wide swath of Middle America infamously known as Tornado Alley. Violent tornado winds brew up regularly along the length and breadth of the plains.

In June 1957, Fargo lost ten of its unfortunate folk to a deadly twister. A month and a half earlier, a series of half-a-dozen tornadoes had touched down near Lubbock, but luckily spared the city.

The dusty one-horse towns around Lubbock were on wary guard for wild weather each spring and summer—but bad weather and bad news could come at any time.

Blizzards that began in Canada or the Dakotas seldom fizzled out until they reached the Texas Panhandle. Even across such a broad expanse of planet, what someone felt in one place would soon surely be felt in the other.

***

Fargo sits along the floodplain of the Red River of the North. The town flourished after the Northern Pacific Railroad drove its last spike in 1871. Lubbock, ironically, was not all that far from the Red River of the South. The Texas town incorporated in 1909, when its first railroad arrived. Although their beginnings were almost 40-years apart, their origins are reasonably similar.

Lubbock is located on the Llano Estacado on the southern plains of the Texas Panhandle. It's an area known for livestock and cotton fields. Cottony white fiber spheres line area roads like snow when harvest arrives, tricking the eyes into believing it's something it's not.

In miles, from Lubbock it's barely a spit in the wind to Turkey, Texas the hometown of Bob Wills. Wills, known as the "King of Western Swing", first appeared with the Light Crust Doughboys and then with his own Texas Playboys. He made famous such country classics as "San Antonio Rose", "Cherokee Maiden", "Steel Guitar Rag", "Texarkana Baby", and "Sugar Moon". Admittedly, it's the music of farmers and ranchers—steel guitars, dobros and fiddles—the downhome music of rural folks. And although Fargo is more than a thousand miles away, its radio stations and local dancehalls enthusiastically played that infectious foot shuffling music too.

Along the length of those windswept plains—Dumas in Texas, Guymon, Dodge City, Kearney, and to Aberdeen in South Dakota, it didn't matter much where a soul was from. Close-knit families pretty much all enjoyed the bouncy melodies that emanated along with annoying cracks, pops, and routine static in the soft glow from the light of living room radios. Be they Texas-bred to the south or of Scandinavian pedigree farther north, impressionable young lads strived to mimic the magical sounds of Wills, Ernest Tubb, Jim Lowe, Bobby Helms, Webb Pierce, Eddie Arnold, Floyd Tillman, Little Jimmy Dickens and Hank Williams—and the rollicking country tunes that vied for time on the local airwaves.

Many of the up-and-coming country singers were now engaged in what was becoming known as *rockabilly* music— popular music with a decidedly country flavor and a rocking beat: Marty Robbins, Johnny Cash, velvet-voiced Jim Reeves, Johnny

Horton, the Everly Brothers, and a cool Memphis hillbilly cat named Presley, were all crossing over from country and making a big splash on the popular music charts—especially now that inexpensive pocket-sized transistor radios were coming into vogue. A fellow could hand jive while out baling hay, souping up his V-8 Ford or while delivering newspapers by bicycle along his route. Popular music was no longer limited to the living room radio.

Not only that, enamored over nasal-voiced country stars, many awestruck young lads were investing a few hard-earned bucks in their own musical instruments. The local Sears and Roebuck made it cheap and easy.

It was dang well certain that down on the dusty plains of Lubbock there wasn't much for a fellow to do but toil and sweat in the summer fields. And up Fargo way young men operated Farmalls or John Deeres in summer and wielded snow shovels come winter.

Come to think of it, with country music being what it was, except for the bitter cold for half the year, Fargo and Lubbock weren't all that much different.

That's pretty much how it was across America's heartland during the middle fifties.

The Music of Bobby Vee

PART ONE

1

HOLLY ON the RISE

For the past few years, a lanky, spectacled young Texan from Lubbock was working at making a minor name on the local music scene. Charles "Buddy" Hardin Holley, now more popularly known as Buddy Holly, had worked hard to break into the music business, playing local radio spots and trifling country gigs. Along with friend Bob Montgomery, he was one-half of a young country and western duo. The boy's had dubbed themselves with a less than imaginative stage moniker of *Buddy and Bob*.

The boys had met at Lubbock's Hutchinson Junior High School in 1949, a dozen blocks south of the burgeoning Texas Tech University. Musically driven, they began primarily playing bluegrass music at local radio shows and school assemblies, steadily building a loyal hometown audience.

Not one to remain satisfied with this minor accomplishment; the innovative Holly soon blended his music with rhythm and blues—which is apparent in his later recordings and homemade demos.

Soon, the two school chums were performing regularly on the area's popular *Sunday Party* radio show, which served to add to their growing popularity.

At age nineteen, Holly already had been introduced to rising fame when on February 13, 1955, the Lubbock native opened at the local Cotton Club for a cool, hip shaking Memphis cat named Elvis Presley. Presley, at the time still with Sun Records, was gaining notoriety almost as much for his outlandish physical gyrations as he was for his music. Excited adolescents flocked to his concerts in droves and with Elvis's appearance at the Cotton Club; Holly was invited to open the show. It went good. In fact, Presley graciously lent his prized Martin guitar to Holly for the show.

Holly opened twice more for Presley that year, as Elvis's celebrity began to catch fire.

Soon, the *Buddy and Bob* experiment folded, with the brief-lived *Buddy and the Two Tones* coming into being and then Holly's band morphed into *The Crickets*. With the addition of the trio of talented musicians, Holly's musical prowess continued to evolve and blossom.

By then Columbia recording star Marty Robbins had acquired considerable clout. He had already scored five country Top Ten records, with the last one being the #1 "Singing the Blues".

Robbins' records had begun to cross over into the pop field and he'd become aware of the lanky, talented young Texan in Lubbock. Robbins' manager Eddie Crandall, had spotted Buddy on a country package show at Lubbock's Fair Park Coliseum, featuring the popular combo of Bill Haley and the Comets.

With Robbins' help and encouragement, Holly soon put pen to paper and signed a Decca recording contract.[1]

After some false starts, on 27 May 1957, the Brunswick label (a Decca Records subsidiary), released the single "That'll Be the Day" by the Crickets (Holly, and band mates Jerry Allison, drums, Joe B. Mauldin, upright bass and Niki Sullivan on rhythm guitar). It wasn't an easy sell, however, as the record languished most of the summer and did not reach the charts until August. Then it took off! With its driving rockabilly beat, the song soared to #1 on the national record charts in late September.

Soon, under his own name without the Crickets, Holly charted his own Top Ten hit, with the infectious "Peggy Sue", released on another Decca subsidiary, Coral Records. The talented

---

[1] Buddy Holly Biography Internet website. Uncredited and undated.

Holly now had major hit records as both a solo artist and as lead singer of the Crickets—he was basically competing against himself for chart placement and airtime. With such success, extensive tours and TV appearances soon followed.

During the remainder of 1957 and the following year, Holly and the Crickets scored additional hits, although only "Oh Boy" reached the Top Ten. In fact, the Crickets' "It's So Easy" and Holly's "Girl On My Mind" failed to chart. Holly's August '58 offering "Heartbeat" only reached #82, nationally.

With his career rocketing along, Holly married Maria Elena Santiago, a receptionist he met at a music publisher's office.[2] In what can only be called a whirlwind romance—more accurately a West Texas tornado—Holly handed her a rose five hours into their first date and proposed. They married two months later in his hometown of Lubbock.

With tensions rising, in November '58, Holly and the original Crickets split up. Coral had other plans for him. Stringed instruments, *à la* violins, and full orchestras would soon supplement and replace simple guitar arrangements, giving his records a sound more appealing to a more mature audience.

His rather sudden marriage to Maria Elena had also created friction between Holly and his manager, Norman Petty. When Holly tried to retrieve his royalties from previous recordings, he found them frozen until a dispute was settled with a New York promoter.

Record sales were slumping, his royalties were on hold, and he had a new wife to care for. With such formidable obstacles facing him, Holly reluctantly signed onto the Winter Dance Party tour—a frigid three-week outing across the upper Midwest in the heart of winter.

He had little desire to embark on such a venture, but he shared the discomfort with other popular figures. Up and coming teen-oriented stars Latino Ritchie Valens, pop/doo wop group Dion

---

[2] Holly met Peermusic publisher receptionist Maria Elena Santiago on a 1958 visit to New York City, was instantly smitten and asked her out. They married two months later, August 15, 1958.

and the Belmonts, J.P. Richardson (AKA The Big Bopper) and Holly's reincarnated, pseudo Crickets—a conglomeration of temporary stand-ins—were also on the bill.

The Winter Dance Party certainly wasn't Holly's dream tour, but money was short and he had a new solo record due out to plug. The songs had been recorded in New York with a stringed orchestra under the guidance of Coral music's Dick Jacobs—one a lovely ballad, the other a bouncy tune penned by a 15-year old Brill Building songwriter by the name of Paul Anka. A few weeks on the road promoting the disc might go a long way to jump-start the record's popularity and bring in some sorely needed cash.

On a bitter January 23, 1959, the entertainers boarded a rickety bus in Milwaukee and set forth on an ill-fated odyssey.

2

VELLINE

In 1892, 18-yr old Christ Velline and his sister came to America from snow-covered mountains and deep, clear fiords of Norway, settling in the flat, pastures of the Upper Midwest. In America, they were now about as far from snow-capped mountains and icy inlets as they could be. During the next few years, Christ engaged in farming and merchandising at various locations in Central and Eastern North Dakota. Eight-years later he married Christine Fimreite Thompson in Fargo, along the North Dakota/Minnesota border. Within three-years they relocated some 60 miles to Buttzville, ND, gained citizenship and opened a general store. He operated the store until 1929, when they moved to Fargo. The couple sired eight children. Among them, Sydney Rolland who was born December 29, 1907. Sydney would grow up and marry Saima Tapanila, remaining in Fargo. The couple produced three sons, William, Sydney Jr. and Robert.

***

Most people who knew them probably agreed the Sydney Velline family of Fargo, North Dakota was musically gifted. The patriarch, Sydney, of Norwegian/Finnish descent, played piano and violin. Young sons Bill and Sydney, Jr. played an array of trumpets and trombones, but became proficient guitarists during their teens. An uncle played saxophone. It was little wonder that baby Robert Thomas Velline, born April 30, 1943, would eventually follow their ancestral lead.

Music in the modest, well-kept wood frame Velline household, if not essential, at the very least provided a necessary respite from Fargo's seemingly endless winters.

While the family entertained inside, Northern lights flickered across the black sky—the aurora borealis conducting its own silent concert—while toasty fires crackled and spit bright orange sparks from neighboring chimneys. The tart smell of wood smoke wafted through the neighborhood, lingering in the cold stillness of the evenings. Snow hung in the air. This was no winter destination for the faint of heart.

With frosty breath clouding the night air, a person strolling by the home might catch a refrain of a favorite popular tune as the young boys took turns harmonizing on frigid Fargo evenings. Little did the talented Velline kids realize the dramatic changes that were in store for their futures.

***

At age 15 young Bobby, by then a proud sophomore member of Fargo's Central High School Marching Band, was playing sax with ample skill. Prowess with the shiny brassy instrument, however, was not the younger Velline boy's primary aspiration. The high school band's uninspired repertoire was mired in standard ensemble pieces, playing pretty much what most every high school band played as they strutted up and down frost-hardened football fields performing lackluster halftime shows for a disinterested audience.

Peppy cheerleaders in bright school colors drummed up midgame enthusiasm as they pranced along the sidelines chanting, while on the gridiron the band rolled out another off-key marching tune.

But rather than parade along the frozen turf with the rest of the band members, saxophonist Bobby Velline wanted to rock out like teen radio favorites: Ricky Nelson, The Diamonds, Larry Williams and duck walking Chuck Berry. Bobby may have been changing out the reed and polishing his shiny instrument before taking to the football field, but it was other tunes that he was humming.

It was perhaps a perfect time for teen-oriented music to emerge. Record formats were changing from the old, brittle 78-rpm discs to the more compact, moderately flexible plastic 45s. Selling for less than a dollar each, they were within the allowance range of many teens. Furthermore, many retailers had begun allowing record rack jobbers to display records within their stores, thus making it much easier for teens to find current hits of the day.

With an influx of newer teen-oriented artists making the scene, steadily slipping into the background were the balladeers of the forties and fifties. Now, guitar virtuosos began to take over the popular record charts. Minnesotan Eddie Cochran was belting out a string of hits with "20 Flight Rock", "Sittin' in the Balcony" and "Summertime Blues". Windsor, Canada's Jack Scott was hitting it big with "My True Love", "Leroy" and "Goodbye Baby". Gene Vincent's "Be-Bop-A-Lula" and "Lotta Love" claimed their share of the charts. Of course there were Presley and Buddy Holly and the Crickets. Finding this infectious new music was only a quick spin of the radio dial away.

In the late fifties, rock and roll was fresh, new, and exciting. That was the musical itch saxophonist Bobby Velline was feeling. It gnawed at him with urgency. A hip, handsome youngster with rock and roll aspirations could only play *Seventy-six Trombones* and *Stars and Stripes Forever* just so many times.

***

In the mid to late 50's, an array of classic crooners such as Frank Sinatra, Tony Martin, Vaughn Monroe, Rosemary Clooney, Perry Como, and others were gradually being ushered aside as the new music trend, rock and roll, began capturing the imaginations of the nation's teenagers. Elvis Presley, Pat Boone, Tommy Sands and Bill Haley were being heard regularly on the radio, as were black artists like Fats Domino and the flamboyant Little Richard.

The dynamic Jackie Wilson was recording contagious melodies like "Reet Petite" and "Lonely Teardrops" thus sending eager teens scurrying to their local record shops. Buddy Knox, from the curiously named town of Happy, Texas had scored a number one record with "Party Doll" and Ersel Hickey had struck pay dirt with "Bluebirds Over the Mountain". Dale Hawkins, rockabilly pioneer born in Gold Mine, Louisiana, discovered his mother lode with swamp rock boogie classic "Susie Q", and

Ronnie Self's raucous "Bop-A-Lena" practically melted his guitar strings!

It was this kind of music that young Bobby Velline aspired to play, not so much the high school band's tired old marches the bandmaster conjured up. As Mitch Miller's[3] tedious "Colonel Bogey" came up for the umpteenth time, Bobby twisted the radio dial hoping the harmonizing Everly Brothers' catchy "Bye Bye Love" would break across the airwaves. The melody was already playing in his head.

***

In 1957, young Canadian-American Paul Anka led the way of the teen heartthrob cadre with his self-penned hit "Diana". This is not to say that Presley, Boone and others weren't setting teen hearts aflutter, because phonograph record, movie ticket and teen magazine sales were ascending rapidly.

During the same year, Dick Clark's *American Bandstand* debuted on the nation's television sets reaching a loyal listening audience that registered in the tens of millions daily. The adolescent oriented broadcast showcased the Top 40 music hits of the day and presented handsome young guest stars for the young teen audience to "ooh", "ahh" and sigh over. Bandstand was the quintessential teen dance show, with a regular lineup of greased pompadour and ponytailed kids bopping wildly to current numbers, while the charming Clark emceed the popular music show.

Along with an often-astounding lineup of current guest performers, the program's Rate-a-Record segments spotlighted new releases that Clark had targeted for success.

Using a scale of 35 to 98, Clark would invite two audience members to preview and "rate" a new record, to which the

---

[3] Mitch Miller was a successful recording industry executive, record producer and conductor who recorded his own hits of "The Yellow Rose of Texas", "March From the River Kwai (Colonel Bogey)" and "The Children's Marching Song", during the 1950s. The Mitch Miller Orchestra recorded several popular albums and Miller hosted the popular television program *Sing Along With Mitch,* from 1961-64. In its own way, it was a precursor to karaoke; as song lyrics appeared at the bottom of the TV screen so that viewers could in fact, sing along.

handsome host averaged the scores. When asked why a particularly high score was given, the rater might often reply with the clichéd remark, "It's got a good beat and it's easy to dance to!" ...and the steady ring of cash registers increased as kids rushed off to buy the new sound of the day.

Most any hip kid who appreciated current music and had access to a 17 inch television set dashed home from school each afternoon to catch Philly's gaggle of sophisticated teen dancers— Pat Molittieri, Carmen and Ivette Jimeniz, Justine and Bob, Kenny Rossi and Arlene occupying the dance floor with their hot new versions of The Stroll, The Walk, and one might even add The Bunny Hop!

Tuning in right after school, one could hear new songs being previewed and see the day's special guests perform in black and white splendor. For many of America's youth *Bandstand* was a weekday ritual and subject for intense conversation in school hallways the next day. In fact, many of the kids knew the show's popular theme song by heart and one could surmise that it regularly popped in and out of their muddled thoughts during tedious history and algebra classes.

Regarding guest appearances, Philadelphia based Swan Records' star Freddy Cannon appeared on *Bandstand* more than 100 times. With popular teen idols like Cannon, Frankie Avalon, Fabian, Connie Francis, Dion and the Belmonts and Annette Funicello leading the way, the only truly memorable artist of the era not appearing on the show was the King himself, Elvis Presley! Megastars Pat Boone, The Platters, Buddy Holly and the Crickets all spent their two-and-a-half minutes in front of the TV cameras lip-syncing whatever their current hit record happened to be.

About this same time, Bobby Velline's older sibling by 5-years, Bill, scrapped the brass instrument he'd been playing and acquired a guitar. He set about teaching himself to play by listening to country guitarists of the day. Before long Bill had become adept with the instrument, picking out chords and rhythm patterns with great confidence and flair.

Bobby soon followed his brother's lead, saving $30 from his paper route delivering the *Fargo Forum* door to door. Without hesitation he invested in an inexpensive Harmony guitar.[4] Through Sears, Roebuck and Company outlets, Harmony had pretty much cornered the market on cheap guitars.

Brother Bill progressed rapidly as a guitarist and soon joined forces with 18-year-old drummer friend Bob Korum and a stubby fingered bass player by the name of Jim Stillman. At Bill's urging and as winter snows melted, they boys held their first band practice in the spring of 1958.

Years later Bobby remarked, "It was more a jam session than a band practice." The friends were simply gathering for fun and had not discussed the possibility of playing in legitimate music venues.

But as amateur as the boys were, they refused to make room for young Bobby, who pestered them relentlessly to allow him to join in. In their minds he was still a kid.

The early jam sessions coincided with Elvis Presley's induction into the U.S. Army on March 24, 1958. Presley was at the height of his popularity with every record and every side racing up the charts and becoming a major hit, when Uncle Sam summoned him. Into the Army Presley went, shedding his sideburns and youthful hairstyle to the cruel fate of an Army barber's clippers.

Seeking no favors, Presley declined enlisting in Special Services and entertaining the troops. He willingly accepted his regular Army role in an infantry unit.

After a stint at the giant central Texas Fort Hood military installation, autumn found Presley unceremoniously shipped

---

[4] In 1892, Wilhelm Schultz founded Harmony, a maker of affordable music instruments. In an attempt to corner the ukulele market, Sears, Roebuck and Co. bought the company in 1916 and became the largest producer in the United States. In 1930, the Chicago-based Harmony sold half-a-million guitars, mandolins, banjos and other stringed instruments. By the late 30s, they began again to sell violins, while continuing to produce Harmony, Sears Silvertone, and products under various other trade names. Harmony Guitar Company ceased operations in 1975. (Wikipedia)

overseas to Germany to sing the "G.I. Blues" both literally and figuratively.

Elvis being temporarily in absentia, other talented heartthrobs like Ricky Nelson were filling the void. It seemed that most every kid who could afford it, or who had the desire, took up a musical instrument—generally that meant guitar.

With little to do until spring arrived, snow melted and the local Class C baseball team took to the field, the music-minded Velline boys hijacked the family basement, working most any song that had a tantalizing rocking beat—Hawkins (Ronnie and Dale), Vincent, Perkins, Presley perhaps some Hank Williams and, of course, those catchy songs "That'll Be the Day" and "Peggy Sue" by the skinny West Texas kid named Holly. The improvised combo strummed and drummed whatever song had that raucous rockabilly[5] sound, as older brother Bill worked his nimble fingers frantically up and down the inexpensive Harmony's fret board.

With the persistence of an adolescent cat after a mouse, Bobby tried wheedling his way into his brother's makeshift band. To the older boys he was a stubborn nuisance and rightly so. At the time, Bobby's yearning was little more than a kid's passing fancy, as he had given no thought to pursuing a music career.

Not to be denied a place with his older siblings, young Bobby teased, cajoled and pleaded, trying every way he could to join in. His annoying resolve eventually earned him a chance to join the jam sessions—with a promise he'd remain quiet. With a threat of banishment from the makeshift band hanging over his head, Bobby tried to keep his promise—at least until he became more deeply ensconced within the group.

But once the band cranked it up, to his boyish surprise, none of the other band members knew the song lyrics. Astonishingly,

---

[5] Rockabilly was an early blending of western country with a dash or rhythm and blues. Many of the early rock and roll pioneers performed rockabilly before refining their music: Presley, Holly, Roy Orbison, Marty Robbins, Johnny Cash, Carl Perkins, Ray Smith, Carl Mann, Conway Twitty, Buddy Knox, Johnny Burnette, Ronnie Hawkins, Dale Hawkins (not related), Ersel Hickey, and scores of others. Even Pat Boone rocked out for a time, before discovering that ballads were his forte.

he did! At the tender age of 15, through default, Bobby became the group's lead singer.

***

Musically, at least regarding rock and roll, there wasn't much happening up Fargo way. Now and then someone of moderate prominence might pass through or a local celeb perform at the Red River Valley Fair. A Pat Boone or Elvis Presley film might spend a weekend at the city cinema or the jukebox servicer stock a machine with a hot new number. But, in general the city could be summed up in that "Fargo was a far go" for any big name star. Up there in the Dakotas, it was about as out-of-the-way as a place could be. Why, even US Highway 2, the final east/west link below the Canadian border, bypassed the city 80-miles to the north.

***

Fargo, the largest city in North Dakota, and Moorhead, Minnesota share the banks of the Red River of the North. It's fertile soil—some of the best in the country. The earth sprouts green fields early with spring wheat and shoots of new barley, sugar beets and beans, then a golden glow emanates in summer from vast saffron fields of sunflowers.

The flat, rich lands of the Red River Valley are prone to flooding from annual snowmelts and blockage from ice dams that form with the spring melts. Snow blows heavy and often up there. It comes early and stays late.

Most of the hearty folks who live across the region are descended from northern European stock, strong people accustomed to hard work and harsh weather. And harsh it was. Long winter nights of -20 degrees and below are not uncommon. The area experiences pleasant green summers, but stark frigid winters.

This is the "Wunnerful, wunnerful" land of renowned band leader Lawrence Welk[6] and pop favorite Norma Deloris

---

[6] Welk was a popular big band leader, accordionist, recording musician and TV host of The Lawrence Welk Show, from the German-speaking community of Strasburg, North Dakota. His brand of music came to be known as "champagne music." He had a habit of praising a song well done with a highly accented "wunnerful, wunnerful!"

Egstrom—far better known as singer Peggy Lee[7]. It's a traditional region with old-fashioned people—and conventional music. Welk, with his heavy European accent, hosted a long-running popular television show featuring big band numbers and an array of talented entertainers that appealed to family audiences—hardly proper fare for the budding guitar virtuosos in the Velline family!

With a lack of sufficient options beyond static-laden radio stations and snowy television channels, the music-appreciating brothers routinely attended local country and western shows; jostling their way through the excited masses at the coliseum and other popular venues. The Velline boys enjoyed the enthusiastic crowds and relished the catchy honky tonk sounds that emanated from twangy guitars, screeching fiddles and melancholy dobros, while adoring couples held closely and scooted across the squeaky dance floor.

"Time will tell if I've..." Lulu Belle and Scotty wailed as the speakers fluttered over the din of the crowd. Now that was music the noisy crowd could appreciate!

Respectfully appreciative and humbly attentive during the local shows, upon its conclusion, the boys rushed home and emulated the performances for father Sydney and mother Saima Tapanila in their small Fargo home. (This may explain Bobby's seemingly natural gift at faithfully covering other artist's material on his albums—often doing better than the original. Although his primary interest was the new rock and roll, live country music was more readily available in the upper Midwest during Bobby's formative music years; after all it was the down-to-earth sound of the nation's farmlands).

Even though they had expressed little interest in performing for others during their impromptu practices, the boys were quite adept at imitating the bands they witnessed.

---

[7] Peggy Lee was an American pop singer, songwriter, actress, and vocalist with Benny Goodman's band. She was born Norma Deloris Egstrom, from Jamestown, North Dakota. She is perhaps most famous for her cover version of "Fever" and her 60's hit, "Is That All There Is?"

But while local country bands were mimicking a purer brand of country as that being written and sung by Hank Thompson, Charlie Walker and Don Gibson, in their basement recitals the Velline boys were going ape and laying down smart licks over rockabilly tunes like "Bird Dog", "Jailhouse Rock" and countryman Johnny Cash's "Ballad of A Teenage Queen". For 15-yr old Bobby Velline, there was no longer any doubt; it was so long sax and goodbye Central High Marching Band.

3

A COLD WINTER

Winter days often hover below zero in the upper Midwest—not below freezing, but below zero!   Nights are worse. Artic snow blasts down across the flat Canadian plains and drifts across barren fields with little to impede its progress. It whisks across narrow highways, clogging roads. Farm machinery deserted in the fields drift over, to remain unseen until spring thaws. Snow drifts high against pastoral farm homes, weathered barns, and decrepit sheds. Electrical cables dangle like umbilical cords from vehicle fronts, a safeguard against fast-freezing temperatures that can cause a car's engine to freeze up in no time. Experienced vehicle operators lug heavy-duty extension cords along so they can plug into outlets that spring up from parking spots like new growth timber. Unforgiving blizzards occur across that part of the country with such predictability that local residents give the storms little thought. Regardless, wise vehicle operators are prepared for winter's onslaught.

It was this kind of brutal situation the busload of youthful, ill-prepared entertainers found themselves in during the winter of 1959; freezing temps, snow, ice, flu and colds, lack of sleep and proper clothing. They were Texans, Californians and city-dwelling New Englanders who were unaccustomed to brutal Midwestern seasons.

These were killer winters that a person could simply not step into unprepared.

The rickety bus barreled on over the icy pavement. Wind howled through cracks around the vehicles' drafty windows. The inadequate heater sputtered, doing little to alleviate the cold inside. The half-frozen travelers huddled closer as the bus ground on. The crunch of tire chains going in the opposite direction mashed icy roads and threw up slushy residue as they passed.

For the past eleven days, the unreliable bus rumbled across the upper Midwest on what was billed as the Winter Dance Party.[8] The package tour would cover twenty-four cities in twenty-four days, beginning on January 23 at George Devine's Ballroom in Milwaukee, Wisconsin and ending February 15 at the Illinois State Armory in Springfield, Illinois. Ohio, Illinois, Wisconsin, Minnesota, Iowa... Some dates found the rickety bus crisscrossing a tired path it had covered only days before.

An icy draft crept along the bus floor chilling the feet of the riders. The chill never seemed to leave. The weary travelers performed each evening in drafty auditoriums then immediately boarded the bus so it could slog on into the dark, snowy nights to the next distant venue.

With this icy weather, one might have wondered if anyone on the bus had given thought to how fitting it was that just a few weeks before Alaska had been admitted as the Union's 49th state. This was as close to Artic weather that many on the bus would ever endure.

With still a couple months left, it had not been a good winter. The day before the bus rolled out of Milwaukee to start the tour, twelve anthracite coal miners had died when water from the icy Susquehanna River broke through and flooded several interconnected galleries of Pennsylvania's River Slope Mine; proof that unexpected tragedy could come at any time.

But in small town America, in the upper Midwest where folks were accustomed to Mother Nature's inconveniences—ice and snow, blizzards and blustery gales—kids enjoyed good times at the skating rinks in Fargo and Morehead. The heavily bundled up bobbysoxers were used to icy weather and transistor radios

---

[8] The Winter Dance Party was a package bus tour across the upper Midwest, crisscrossing Wisconsin, Iowa, Illinois and Minnesota, a 24-day tour, during the harsh winter season of 1959. Buddy Holly and The Crickets headlined the tour, with Dion and the Belmonts, Ritchie Valens, a portly J.P. Richardson (AKA the Big Bopper), Frankie Sardo and some musicians (including a then unknown Waylon Jennings) making up the show.

Robert Reynolds

blasted out the latest pop hits as skaters cut across the ice. Soon, one of the biggest music variety shows of the winter would come cruising in for one highly anticipated evening of rock and roll. It was an exciting time.

Back on the drafty tour bus, as it clanked and shuddered along, snow sputtered and blew in flurries, at best—and it blew with fury, at worst as the shivering entertainers grumbled and complained. It was the worst time of the year to be traveling the area.

23

The Music of Bobby Vee

4

A FRIGID TOUR

A time of sock hops, pompadours and saddle shoes, popular radio in 1957 and '58 was broadcasting wide-ranging ditties like "Talk to Me", "Mountain of Love", "Come Go With Me", "Rebel Rouser" and "Smoke Gets in Your Eyes", "Teenager in Love", and "Lavender Blue". Along with Elvis Presley's raucous gyrating to "Hound Dog", "Don't Be Cruel", "All Shook Up" and "Treat Me Nice", there came a softer touch with the mellow tones of crooner Pat Boone.[9] Rock and roll was spreading it around and there was an acceptable sound for everyone's taste.

But along with the giants of the industry, Presley and Boone, The Platters and Duane Eddy, others had emerged onto the national music scene. One in particular, was the lanky, spectacled young man from West Texas, Buddy Holly. His nasal pitched, Texas drawl, self-penned energetic rockabilly songs like "That'll Be the Day" (inspired by a spoken line from the John Wayne film, *The Searchers*) had captured the airwaves. Holly and his pals The Crickets had scored individually and collectively, already breaking the Top Ten three times. But in the middle of winter 1959, a shivering Holly found himself chilled, perhaps in the first throes of

---

[9] In the early days of rock and roll, only Elvis Presley rivaled and surpassed Pat Boone's success. Boone began as a rocker, repeatedly charting hits in 1955 by mostly covering R&B hits of the day—Fat's Domino's "Ain't That A Shame" (#1), and The El Dorado's "At My Front Door (Crazy Little Mama)" (#7). But in 1956 he scored another #1 with a slower number, Ivory Joe Hunter's "I Almost Lost My Mind". Several number one's followed, including medium tempo "Don't Forbid Me", "Love Letters in the Sand", "April Love" and 1961's "Moody River". With few exceptions (his 1962 novelty tune "Speedy Gonzales" #6), Boone discovered gold with his ballads and seldom returned to the rocking days. A rarity among young entertainers, by the time Boone began his prolonged stay on popular record charts he was long-time married to Shirley Lee Foley, daughter of country and western heavyweight Red Foley. Pat Boone scored 18 Top Ten single records and 10 Top Twenty albums (including his "April Love" and "State Fair" soundtracks—both charting at #12). He was second only to Presley as the biggest charting artist in the late 50's. His accomplishments as a singer, actor, writer and television personality are unequalled. It's claimed that Elvis called Pat Boone one of his favorite singers. In 1977, daughter Debbie Boone's hit song, "You Light Up My Life" spent an unheard of 10 weeks at #1 on Billboard's Hot 100 chart!

influenza, and a thousand miles away from his cozy Lubbock home.

While members of the Velline brothers' still anonymous group were honing their instrumental skills in the frigid Fargo winter of '59, the Winter Dance Party bus tour rumbled on through freezing days and colder nights.

With icy winds blowing in off Lake Superior, January 31 found the youthful showmen entertaining an enthusiastic crowd at the Duluth Armory. The bus had arrived after a long haul from Fort Dodge, Iowa, 368 grueling miles along monotonous two-lane frozen highways. In the audience to see Holly and the rest of the singers on the bill was a high-schooler who had come over from the gritty iron-range town of Hibbing, some 75-miles away. Holly's performance enthralled an impressionable young Robert Zimmerman, who would briefly tour with an as yet unnamed group from Fargo[10]—but that was still a ways off.

With nighttime temperatures ranging from about -5 to -10 degrees below zero and daytime temperatures barely reaching a +6 degree high there was little wonder the tour entourage was coming to its wit's end.[11]

Although the West Coast of the U.S. was experiencing extremely warm January temperatures, International Falls, Minnesota was having the coldest and snowiest January on record. (January, for example, showed Los Angeles and San Francisco experiencing their warmest period while Muskegon, Michigan and International Falls were having the coldest--and Muskegon's snowiest January of all time). NOAA, the National Oceanic and Atmospheric Administration reported: "Extreme cold early in

---

[10] Robert Zimmerman, AKA Elston Gunn, joined the Shadows, albeit briefly. Claiming he'd come off tour with Conway Twitty (who was then still a rock and roller having recently struck #1 with "It's Only Make Believe"). Zimmerman, however, had only attended a Twitty concert. An adequate keyboard player, The Shadows took him on believing he could add depth to their music. Unfortunately Zimmerman/Gunn had no piano and the boys couldn't afford to buy one, so there was a mutual and amiable parting. Zimmerman/Gunn resurfaced a few years later, finding mega stardom under a new stage name, Bob Dylan.
[11] (From the Minneapolis/St Paul Air Port, weather history,
http://www.wunderground.com/history/airport/KMSP/1959/1/31/DailyHistory.html?req_city=&req_state=&req_statename=&reqdb.zip=&reqdb.magic=&reqdb.wmo=)

January accompanied a front, which dropped daily temperatures as much as 50' and was responsible for a weekly average temperature of 20' 1..." Regardless of the extreme weather conditions, when the Winter Dance Party bus rolled in with its bevy of big-name entertainers, crowds were large and enthusiastic at the upper Midwest venues.

***

In the snowy bleakness, the rickety bus pulled away from the Duluth Armory after the show and barreled south into the freezing Wisconsin night. Holly historian Bill Griggs[12], believed that as many as five different reconditioned buses were used during the tour, each one less reliable than the one it replaced. The vehicle's inadequate heater had caused some members of the touring group to come down with frostbite—perhaps the most notable victim was Carl Bunch, Holly's drummer. Others were heavily fatigued from sleeping upright in the worn out old bus's tattered seats, teeth chattering from the cold, and with dirty clothing hanging in the aisles, as they rolled across seemingly endless miles through snow and ice.

Members of the various headlining groups—Buddy Holly and the Crickets (The original Crickets were back in Lubbock. Holly had taken on Waylon Jennings, Carl Bunch and Tommy Allsup as his makeshift Crickets for the tour. The four of them had left New York by train to meet up in Chicago with the rest of the show members.) New Yorkers Dion and the Belmonts (on the strength of their trio of singles for fledgling Laurie Records' "I Wonder Why", "No One Knows" and "Don't Pity Me"), Southern Californian Ritchie Valens ("Donna", "La Bamba" and "Come On, Let's Go") and South Texan J.P. Richardson, AKA The Big Bopper ("Chantilly Lace") were experiencing a variety of ills— colds, flu, frostbite, and insomnia. If there was a malady, someone on the bus probably had it. To make matters worse for Holly, he

---

[12] Founder of the Buddy Holly Memorial Society, William "Bill" Griggs was unquestionably the foremost authority and historian of Buddy Holly and the Crickets. A New Englander by birth, Griggs moved to Lubbock in 1981 to continue his research on the West Texas legend. Griggs died March 29, 2011.

and his manager Norman Petty, who was back in Clovis, were bickering via long-distance.

Forty-one years later Dion (Dimucci) reminisced about the tour in his song "Hug My Radiator"[13], memories of the decrepit old bus lunging into the icy days and cold black nights. It wasn't all bitter memories for him and he'd later remark about his fondness for Holly and their sharing blankets and stories on cold legs of the journey—Dion telling tales about the Bronx, Holly about west Texas—as the bus rattled along. He also tells of the two of them harmonizing—Dion's Bronx blues and Buddy's western drawl blending into something special, unheard before and not heard of again. Years later Dion gave tribute to their friendship with his song "Every Day (that I'm with you)"[14] from the same *Deja Nu* CD.

The bus chugged on over the icy roads of Wisconsin toward Iowa. Many members of the entourage were ready for the tour to end and they were counting the days until their last performance. On their way to Appleton and Green Bay, Wisconsin, for two Sunday shows, the weary old vehicle ground to a halt, stranding the entertainers along the road surrounded by snow and a dense Wisconsin forest.

Fifty-years on from that tragic night, Pamela Huey of the Minneapolis Star Tribune wrote, "as the temperature plunged to around 30 below and the wind howled, fate intervened. The southbound bus creaked to a stop as it struggled up an incline on Hwy 51 about 10 miles south of Hurley.

"Buddy Holly, the Big Bopper, Ritchie Valens, Waylon Jennings, Dion and the others were stranded on a remote highway in the northern Wisconsin forest. They huddled under blankets and burned newspapers to try to stay warm. Buddy's drummer was nursing painful frozen feet."[15]

---

[13] "Hug My Radiator"—track #2 from Dion's 2000 ACE Compact Disc *Deja Nu.*
[14] "Every Day (That I'm With You)"—track #9 from Dion's 2000 ACE Compact Disc *Deja Nu.*
[15] Buddy Holly: The tour from hell. Pamela Huey, (Minneapolis) Star Tribune, February 3, 2009.

The stranded assemblage spent the night in the small town of Hurley, Wisconsin, along Michigan's Upper Peninsula border, then caught a train or Greyhound bus 220 miles to Green Bay, the Appleton show having been cancelled.

Frigid as it was, Monday was to be a much-appreciated free day, but Clear Lake was booked at the last minute. What the travelers had hoped would result in a brief respite turned into another agonizing 355-mile ride back to Iowa.

Holly and many of the others were ready for the nightmarish tour to end. All the seemingly mindless crisscrossing routes and frigid nights of sleeping sitting up had turned the group into a haggard bunch. Some were already contemplating going their own way. Holly especially was ready to leave the drafty bus behind. He had no desire to make the 365-mile ride to Moorhead and was scheming to get there ahead of the rest. An early arrival to the Fargo/Moorhead area might at least give a few of the young men pause to launder their clothing or at least to regain some warmth and rest.

With the original Crickets back in Texas, as yet undiscovered Waylon Jennings, along as Holly's bassist, later wrote, "It was so cold on the bus that we'd have to wear all our clothes, coats and everything…"[16] The bone chilling cold was especially difficult for the Texans and Southern Californian Valens who'd left his coat behind in a rather balmy Pacific climate.

Even though he had taken to wearing multiple pairs of socks, the pain in his frostbitten feet had become unbearable; drummer Carl Bunch left the tour early to be hospitalized in Ironwood, Michigan. Furthermore, influenza had spread among the disheartened entertainers. The Belmonts, Angelo D'Aleo, Carlo Mastrangelo and Fred Milano, had taken to lighting newspapers to generate extra warmth. Without a drummer, Dion, Buddy and Ritchie took turns banging out a rhythm on the drums for each other. As the adage goes, "the show must go on."

---

[16] Deseret New: The Day the Music Died: Buddy Holly, February 3, 1959. Pamela Huey, (Minneapolis) Star Tribune, January 30, 2009.

Their tour bus broken down, it was replaced by a school bus for the next leg of the journey. Less than halfway through the tour, under miserable conditions, the disenchanted entertainers were becoming rebellious.

February 2, originally set as an off date, was rescheduled for Clear Lake, Iowa—a makeup for the cancelled Appleton stop. Tour promoters had called Carroll Anderson, manager of Clear Lake's Surf Ballroom offering him the show. It was a good opportunity to bring in some big name talent so Anderson accepted. The show ran that night from 8 p.m. to 12 a.m. with an admission cost of $1.25 per head. It was good for the Surf Ballroom and ardent fans, but like the others aboard the bus, Holly was displeased.

At last giving in to his impulses to hurry the trek along, Holly decided to charter a flight to the next scheduled stop on the tour, Moorhead, MN. He had no desire to spend another 360-mile night on the bus.

Minutes after finishing the show at the Surf Ballroom in Clearlake, a 1947 V-tailed single-engine Beech Bonanza carrying Buddy Holly, J.P. Richardson (professionally known as the Big Bopper—who was nursing the Flu), Ritchie Valens and 21 year old pilot Roger Peterson lifted off from the small airport in Mason bound for the Fargo/Moorhead area. At 12:55 a.m. light snow was falling and wind blowing as the plane taxied down the icy runway and lifted off.[17]

Meanwhile 370 miles north, bundled against wintry cold, the Velline boys anxiously awaited the arrival of the first true rock and roll show to come to town. They could hardly wait to hear "That'll Be the Day" sung by the star himself.

---

[17] The stories vary about how Ritchie Valens ended up on the plane. Rather than debate how this came about, I have simply opted to report that these were the people aboard the plane.

5

AN UNFORESEEN BEGINNING

Five miles from the Mason City Municipal Airport, with light snow falling, the chartered four-seater plane crashed into a snow-covered cornfield instantly killing all aboard.

Word of the downed plane spread quickly as radio stations began broadcasting the bitter news.

Sid was the first in the Velline family to hear the fateful broadcast and relayed it to his sophomore student brother while home for lunch.

Bobby's first instinct was there must be a misunderstanding. A plane crash? How could that be? The Winter Dance Tour entourage was traveling by bus. Downed in an Iowa cornfield? It couldn't happen. Besides, Bobby already had his ticket for the show...

But the radio kept repeating the gloomy bulletin. Mason, Iowa... Ritchie Valens. J.P. Richardson... Buddy Holly... It came as a shock, as it did to most all of Holly's fans. Word spread quickly through the local high school. Many of the students had planned to attend the show and chatter was brisk. Later that day, Dick Clark opened his Tuesday afternoon American Bandstand TV show with the somber news. The show's dancers in faraway Philadelphia didn't seem so lively that afternoon.

The local *Fargo Forum and Moorhead News* headlined their daily newspaper "3 Rock 'n' Roll Stars Killed In Plane Crash".

The other members of the Winter Dance Party entourage were stunned when they arrived in Moorhead, across the Red River from Fargo, and learned of the tragedy.

With three of the four main headliners now gone, the Winter Dance Party tour was in jeopardy of having to shut down. Heads were put together and a decision made to find local talent to temporarily fill in until known entertainers could be booked to finish out the tour.[18]

A call went out from the show's sponsor, Fargo radio station KFGO, soliciting talented stand-ins.

As word got around, a local Fargo group featuring fifteen-year-old Robert Velline volunteered and was invited to the auditorium. The group, formed only shortly before the tragic accident, had been rehearsing Holly songs—as they had songs of Elvis Presley, The Everly Brothers and others. Young Bobby Velline performed as the lead singer almost by default, primarily because he knew the words to all the songs. They had never performed in front of a real audience.

Although it took some convincing to get talented older brother Bill to go along, the call for help did not go unheeded by the Velline brothers and their band mates. Soon, Jim Stillman called Disc Jockey Charlie Boone who told him to have the band at the auditorium by 7 p.m. There was no audition. All they needed to do was show up.

School let out in midafternoon thus leaving them only four hours to prepare. With thoughts of math and history far from their minds, the boys hurried downtown and bought matching sleeveless sweaters and angora neckties at the local J.C. Penney store. If they sounded as good as they looked, they would be a big hit. (Some sources recall the sweaters being bought at the J.C. Penney store and others remember it being Anthony's, a local department store).

On very short notice the boys hustled to the auditorium and tried to get organized before the curtain went up. In the confusion, Bill Velline had forgotten his guitar strap so Dion graciously loaned out his. With heavy hearts over the loss of Buddy Holly and the others, Bobby and the nervous new combo readied themselves to go on stage.

---

[18] Shortly, teen heartthrobs Frankie Avalon, Fabian (Forte) and Jimmy Clanton replaced the show's three fallen stars. By then, the three substitutes were stars in their own right, Avalon having scored big with "De De Dinah", "Ginger Bread" and his #1 hit "Venus", Fabian with "I'm A Man", and Clanton with "Just A Dream". Sardo, Dion and the Belmonts and the faux Crickets continued and finished out the tour.

Boone scheduled them to go on second, following Buddy's stand-in bass player Waylon Jennings, who did a short set recognizing the fallen stars. There's some disagreement over who actually went first as some reports claim it was Jennings' while others say Frankie Sardo, an original member of the tour group, went first and sang Ritchie Valens' hit "Donna". Bobby remembers Jennings opening the show with the Valens' song.

During the short break, Charlie Boone then appeared on stage.

"What's your name?" Boone turned and asked Bobby.

The boys hadn't thought it out, so on the spur of the moment Bobby blurted their impromptu moniker. Charlie Boone turned to the audience and announced, "Ladies and gentlemen, The Shadows!"[19]

In their brief twenty-minute set, the boys strummed out some up-tempo hits of the day—although Bobby later admitted that he didn't remember the set list. He did however remember being very nervous as he stepped forward to sing before the large crowd.

Bassist Dick Dunkirk would say years later "we only knew six songs that we had rehearsed, so we came down to the show and did six songs."[20]

That evening, 15-year-old Bobby Velline did most of the vocalizing for the group. Some recall Bobby singing "Bye Bye Love" and "Long Tall Sally". He knew the lyrics to "That'll Be the Day", but he didn't sing it that evening. Perhaps they did some Elvis. Perhaps they did some Everly Brothers. The boys were happy to get a chance to play, but certainly not under these circumstances. Bill strummed. Jim thumped his bass. Korum pounded his drum. Bobby wailed. Then, almost suddenly, The Shadows' set was over and they relinquished the stage to a

---

[19] The Day Buddy Holly Died: Bobby Vee Remembers by James M. Tarbox, Knight-Ridder Newspapers, March 29, 1985

[20] Quote extracted from internet interview, Pioneer Public TV, Postcards: Bobby Vee and the Shadows: Family and Friends. May 14, 2012.

youngster of 8 or 9 who sang Laurie London's "He's Got the Whole World In His Hands". It was a melancholy evening.

The newly dubbed Shadows may not have stolen the show but they fared well enough to be called back for a second set near the end of the evening. They repeated the six songs they knew as their encore. For a time at least, the crowd could forget the tragedy that had befallen the show's original entertainers.

At the end of the show, Bing Bengtsson, owner of a local drive-in, handed the boys a business card and offered to manage the group and get them more gigs. Bengtsson also booked bands for high school dances and other events. It didn't take the newly christened Shadows long to decide in the affirmative and accept his offer.

According to Charlie Boone, The Shadows weren't the best band he had worked with, but they were persistent, showing up soon after the Winter Dance Party show to express their interest in cutting a record. But, as eager as they were, that opportunity did not immediately come for the boys.

The Dance Party show being their only brief résumé performance, The Shadows played their first paying gig on Valentine's Day 1959. In fact, a few weeks after their debut Moorhead volunteer appearance; they got their own taste of the travails of a winter mini tour. With temperatures hovering near zero and a dysfunctional heater in an old Oldsmobile, the young musicians drove 45 miles to Breckenridge, MN, with Bobby cradling the bass in his lap in the backseat. They arrived to find their stage to be a series of wooden benches pushed together for a makeshift platform. With ponytailed girls and slicked back boys dancing up a storm, it wasn't long before the rambunctious teens had rock and rolled the benches apart, sending the band's amplifiers crashing to the floor. The engagement paid $60—an amount The Shadows considered a very handsome sum.

Soon, Charlie Boone, who Dee Jayed "Platter Parties" throughout the area, began taking the boys along to play their instruments between the records he spun. Needless to say, their popularity was on the rise.

***

Winter melted into spring and temperatures began to warm.

On April 30, Bobby's 16th birthday, Joe Saad, regional promotional man for Liberty Records caught a Shadows performance at a Fargo drive-in theater. Greatly impressed with Bobby's singing prowess, Saad sent a raw tape of "Suzie Baby", a song written by Bobby during study hall, to Thomas "Snuff" Garrett, a rising Liberty record producer—but nothing came of it. Although Garrett was barely older then The Shadows, he was already considered an old pro as a record producer

Encouraged by Fargo area DJ Scott Beach, Bobby and the Shadows made their way to Minneapolis to record a few sides for Soma Records[21] in the early summer.

During the session at Amos Heilicher's Kay Bank Studios the boys recorded four tracks[22]: "Flyin' High" (an instrumental written by Bill Velline); the Buddy Holly inspired "Suzie Baby"; "Lonely Love"; and "Love Must Have Passed Me By" (Written by Bobby). The boys coughed up $500 for the three-hour morning session and received 1,000 singles.

The session produced Bobby's superb regional smash hit "Suzie Baby", which Heilicher issued across the upper Midwest.[23] The Shadow's guitar driven instrumental "Flyin' High", written by Bill, graced the record's other side.

But with success on the horizon, bass man Stillman dropped out of the group. Dick Dunkirk, whose mother was a staff singer

---

[21] The Soma label was established in 1954 by Amos Heilicher—SOMA being Amos spelled backwards. The small regional label recorded mostly country and western, jazz and polka music, however, it was also a major record distributor throughout the upper Midwest. The label went on to produce or distribute "Mule Skinner Blues" #5 by the Fendermen Recorded on Cuca Record label and distributed nationally by SOMA; "Liar, Liar" by the Castaways #12 in 1965; "Surfin' Bird" by The Trashmen, #4 in 1963 on the Garrett label, also distributed by SOMA—among several other major hits.

[22] The three vocal tracks recorded at Kay Bank Studios in June 1959 exhibit the enormous potential Bobby (Vee) Velline had, even then with so little experience. The songs can be found on the 1995 compact disc *Bobby Vee and the Shadows: The Early Rockin' Years*, Cema Special Products, 5028-2.

[23] Along with owning Kaybank Studios and the Soma label, Amos Heilicher became one of the largest record distributors in the United States. He also went on to own the Musicland record store chain and in engage in jukebox distribution.

on WDAV Radio, replaced him. Dunkirk was 19 and had been playing string bass in a jazz trio, but switched to electric bass when he joined the Shadows. Soon, the Shadows were one of the most requested new bands in the Fargo area.

Shortly, while visiting Sam's Record Land in Fargo, Bill Velline met a piano playing kid from the small Iron Range town of Hibbing, MN. He had driven from Hibbing to see the Winter Dance Party show in Duluth a few nights before Holly's tragic ending. The kid was working as a busboy at the local Red Apple Café and introduced himself as Elston Gunnn—with three "n"s!

Gunnn claimed to have just gotten off tour with Conway Twitty. Twitty[24], at the time was still a major name in rock and roll and had recently performed in the Minneapolis area. It would later be learned that Gunnn had not played for Twitty—he had only seen him perform. This was not the only false claim the young man made.

The Shadows auditioned the young piano player at the KFGO studio and took him aboard. Bill Velline would remark, "he rocked out pretty good in the key of C".[25] They soon found out that "the key of C" was about the only key he could play in.

Confident and fun-loving, joining in spontaneously with handclaps and adding his voice to background vocals when the piano wasn't working out, Gunnn was having a great time as The Shadows' popularity grew.

Elston Gunnn, AKA Robert Zimmerman, played with The Shadows for a very brief period as they made the rounds of area concert and dance halls. Gunnn didn't have a piano and the band didn't have the money to buy one. The association was short-lived and soon Gunnn left to attend college at the University of Minnesota and then moved on to New York City's Greenwich

---

[24] Conway Twitty (real name Harold Jenkins) had come off a number one hit with "It's Only Make Believe". He continued to perform rock and roll and register hit records into 1962, (often up-tempo versions of old standards like "Danny Boy" and "Mona Lisa") but he was not satisfied with the direction his music was taking him. Twitty eventually stepped away from rock and roll and began his career anew by singing only country music. By 1968 Twitty had distanced himself from his earlier R&R hits and began a long period where he was one of country's biggest and most consistent stars.

[25] Quote extracted from the Bob Dylan Encyclopedia and several other sources

Village. He was not fired from the band, as is popularly believed in some circles. It was an amicable parting.

Sometime later Bobby Velline explained simply about Zimmerman/Gunn's brief stay with the band, "it just didn't work out." Oh, and Zimmerman/Gunn's other alias? Bob Dylan.

***

Foreseeing a busy schedule in his future, Robert Thomas Velline withdrew from Fargo Central High School in May 1959.[26] One thing was certain; he had closed the door on any future marches across frozen high school football fields. But little did he know at the time where and how far his journeys would take him.

***

During the late summer at a dance at the Pavilion in Detroit Lakes, MN handsome young Bobby met Karen Bergan, his future bride to be. Unlike his idol Buddy Holly who quickly married upon meeting Maria Elena, Bobby's courtship of Karen lasted for several years before they wed.

***

Summer faded and Northern Minnesota's slippery elm and yellow birch, bur oak and black ash, began to turn to brilliant reds and golds of autumn, setting the forests ablaze in color. There was fire in the forests and fire in the regional record charts, as the boys' debut disc shot up the charts.

The boys pushed the record hard, with Bing Bengtsson coming up with a promotional contest to "Win a date on the town with Bobby Vee", by writing in 25 words or less why the person believed she could be the girl that Bobby sang of. The entry had to be at the radio station no later than July 12.

Bobby later remarked with a smile, "I picked her up in my '53 Oldsmobile. We went out for dinner and I dropped her off at home and that was it."[27]

---

[26] Fargo School District personnel furnished confirmation of withdrawal from high school, via email response.

[27] Quote taken from an uncredited Bobby Vee interview posted on You Tube.

Prize winning dates or not, "Suzie Baby" moved up the singles' charts across Minnesota, Wisconsin, and the Dakotas.

It had begun to break in several scattered markets, getting airplay here and there, but as yet, nothing like the attention it was getting across the upper reaches of the Midwest frontier. It was the first rock and roll record from the Minneapolis area to crack *Billboard's* music charts

Shortly, Kaybank found the boys back in the studio cutting several more sides: "It's Too Late", "Remember the Day", and the beautiful ballad "Laurie"—a sign of what was soon to come.

Within a few months of its release "Suzie Baby", Bobby's study hall composition which he had penned in the "Peggy Sue" vein, climbed to number one on most radio stations in the upper Midwest.

The strength of the song's showing across the region had major record companies showing interest.

Mega-record-companies like Columbia, Capitol and Roulette were clamoring to sign the youngster(s) from Fargo. Jimmy Bowen[28], a fledgling record producer and mildly successful singer himself, encouraged the boys to sign with Roulette[29]. Both he and Buddy Knox had produced hit singles for the company. However, Charlie Boone steered the boys away from Roulette, which had a questionable record of mistreating its artists.[30]

Within the entertainment industry, the late 50's was an era of quiz show scandals, crooked managers, unpaid royalties and payola[31] which entangled such high profile record industry giants as Alan Freed, Tom Clay, Murray "the K" Kaufman, Dick Clark and the crew over at Roulette headed by Morris Levy—among

---

[28] Bowen scored a Top 20 record in 1957 with "I'm Stickin' With You". The record achieved a Gold disc for selling over a million copies, topping out at #14.

[29] Roulette Records was a major record producer and distributor with purported ties to the New York mob. Over the years, Roulette hosted a stable of best selling artists including Jimmy Bowen, Buddy Knox, Ronnie Hawkins, Jo Ann Campbell, Dave "Baby" Cortez, Lou Christie, Jimmie Rodgers, Joey Dee and the Starlighters and later, Tommy James and the Shondells.

[30] For a major Roulette artist's perspective on this subject, read *Me, the Mob, and the Music* by Tommy James, with Martin Fitzpatrick. A Scribner book, February 2010, ISBN 978-1-4391-2865-7.

[31] *Payola* was a phrase coined to identify disk jockeys, record suppliers and others involved offering/receiving bribes or kickbacks for a disk jockey to push certain songs on their shows.

many others. At least twenty-five program directors and DJs were caught up in the scandal.[32]

At Boone's urging, it was the smaller Liberty Records that won the battle for Bobby Vee and the Shadows.

Liberty certainly wasn't the biggest or most glamorous company vying for their talents, but the label was amassing a highly competent stable of consistent hit makers and its reputation for treating its people fairly helped win the boys over. The agreement would continue for the band until 1963, when brother Bill tired of the grueling road trips and the Shadows left the label. As strictly a solo entity, Bobby would continue his relationship with the Liberty label for another ten years.

Banking on the popularity of "Suzie Baby" in the Midwest, Liberty released the song nationally. It showed promise across various regions, doing well in certain markets like Boston, Cleveland and San Diego, where it would become the #12 song for the entire year. The record did not catch on nationally, but it did reach a respectable #77 on the national charts.

As many entertainers are wont to do, Bobby shortened his name from Velline to a more recognizable *Vee*. He was far from being the first teen idol to make such a change and assume a different stage name. Dion and Fabian dropped mention of their last names entirely. Bobby Ridarelli became Bobby Rydell. Charles Westover became Del Shannon. Harry Webb became Cliff Richard. Joseph DiNicola became Joey Dee (of Starlighters fame). Johnny Ramistella became Johnny Rivers. Francesco Castelluccio wisely dropped that tongue twister of a moniker to perform as Frankie Valli. (Also briefly having used Valley).

Beyond any doubt, Bobby's vocals were the band's principal attribute and Liberty relegated the Shadows' name to the second tier on the paper record labels: **BOBBY VEE and THE SHADOWS.**

---

[32] From the internet article entitled Payola: http://www.history-of-rock.com/payola.htm

The group would remain "The Shadows" only briefly.[33] In England, Cliff Richard's backing group The Drifters had come to realize America already had a very popular rhythm and blues group that had recently made inroads into the pop scene. The Drifters records "There Goes My Baby" had climbed to #2 and "Dance With Me" to #15 in 1959. Rather than create confusion over the identical names, Richard's group changed its name to The Shadows. For basically the same reason, Vee's group soon capitulated and changed its name to The Strangers. It was a wise decision, as England's original Shadows would continue on to become one of the most popular, prolific and successful guitar-based bands in the history of rock.

Buoyed by the moderate hit "Suzie Baby", Bobby's first Liberty recording session came on January 7, 1960. It was a split session shared with Johnny Burnette, with both artists being allotted an hour and a half. During his time slot, Burnette recorded "Dreamin'", which soon became a #11 hit. Bobby, on the other hand, recorded "What Do You Want", which barely crept into the Top 100 at #93. He said later that he had no special feeling for "What Do You Want" and wished instead he had recorded the Burnette song as he felt from the beginning that "Dreamin'" would be a hit.

Now, under Tommy "Snuff" Garrett's meticulous guidance, stringed instruments would be featured more prominently on future recordings, "strings" more accurately meaning violins as opposed to guitars.

Bobby's early Liberty recordings beyond "Suzie Baby", which garnered moderate national airplay, did not fare well, barely hovering around number 100 on the national record charts. Songs like the cover version of Adam Faith's number one UK hit, "What

---

[33] England's Shadows (originally Hank Marvin, Bruce Welch, and Brian Bennett (core members), with Jet Harris, Tony Meehan, John Rostill, Ian Samwell, John Farrar and others passing in and out of the band at times) had dubbed themselves The Drifters. But after learning of the popular American Rhythm and Blues group The Drifters, they became The Shadows in the autumn of '59. England's Shadows racked up five #1singles and 17 Top Ten singles in their homeland, plus an array of top hits throughout Europe/Australia/New Zealand. They also scored 4 number 1 LPs and 2 number 2's in the UK.

Robert Reynolds

Do You Want" and its follow-up "One Last Kiss" did not catch on for Bobby with the record buying public, although the latter was certainly worthy of a much higher chart position. The tune was from a scene in the 1960-61 Broadway production *Bye Bye Birdie*. A few years later the play would be made into a movie starring Ann-Margret, Bobby Rydell and Dick Van Dyke. But, as good as the song was, Bobby Vee's "One Last Kiss" dropped all the way to #112. His career appeared mired like a disabled bus in a Fargo snow drift.

With his career stuck in neutral and now being back home in Fargo, the boys started their own small label, aptly named *Vee Records*. Their initial release for the new label was "What'll I Do"; backed by "Leave Me Alone"[34], which featured Bill Velline's Johnny Cash inspired vocals. While Bill took to the mic, Bobby slipped on his older brother's Fender Jazzmaster, stood aside and flailed away. The record fared well; being a Top 5 hit in many of the upper Midwest markets where the band played, as they again made their rounds of area ballrooms. Bill, however, preferred being in the background and it was his sole record as the front man.

Barely more than a year after Buddy Holly's untimely passing, Garrett, who had grown up in Dallas (dropping out of South Oak Cliff High School in the 10th grade), Dee Jayed in Wichita Falls and Lubbock, and was a friend of Buddy Holly, flew with Bobby to Norman Petty's Recording Studios[35] in Clovis, NM—the same studios that had given rise to Holly and the Crickets' first big hits. The boys made their way from Fargo by train.

---

[34] "Leave Me Alone", was composed and produced by Bobby Vee, Vee Records VR 1001 and released February 20, 1960. Most of the other Vee Label recordings were instrumentals.
[35] The Norman Petty Recording Studio is located at 1313 W. 7th Street, Clovis, New Mexico. Right next door is Petty's newer building NorVaJak Music, Inc. that he used for his music publishing operation. NorVaJak is derived from NORman, VA (a shortening of Petty's wife Violet Anne), and JAK (for Jack Vaughn). Ref: Norman Petty Studios – Buddy Holly, Roy Orbison, Waylon Jennings, and The Story of Legendary Texas Music by Randy Jones, April 25, 2011.

Petty was himself a recording artist of significant importance beyond releasing popular recordings by other artists. His Norman Petty Trio scored a half-million seller in 1956 with "Mood Indigo".[36]

Unhindered by union rules and wages, Petty allowed artists using his Clovis studios to spend as much time as they needed until their music was satisfactory. He enforced no time limit on their recording sessions and the results were highly successful.

Garrett's objective in Clovis was for Bobby and The Shadows to record half-a-dozen rockers then fly to Los Angeles to record six more songs with orchestral backing, for an LP entitled *Bobby Vee Sings Your Favorites*. At Snuff Garrett's insistence, Bobby and the boys would record six oldies, not the new, original songs that Bobby had hoped for.

Among others, the boys ripped into recent R&R standards "That'll Be the Day", "White Silver Sands", "Party Doll", "Bye, Bye Love", "Susie Q" and "Butterfly"—all previous hits of the era by other artists. But while they were there, Garrett coaxed out one more tune—a cover of Buddy Holly's wistful "Wishing". It was the only song among the group that had not previously been a big hit. Even Holly's original version would not be released during his lifetime. With the rock and roll half of the album finished, Bobby and Snuff headed for L.A.

But there was a surprise in store when they arrived in California. The orchestral offerings were so captivating that Garrett scrapped the Clovis songs and went with an LP entirely of lush ballads, replete with strings. The album would consist of a dozen reworking's of recent chart-toppers like "It's All In the Game", "My Prayer", and "Young Love". The young singer did such an admirable job on his cover versions of the songs that it was apparent he could equal or often surpass the originals!

---

[36] Besides 1956's popular "Mood Indigo", The Norman Petty Trio also hit big in 1957 with the #18, "Almost Paradise". The Norman Petty Trio with Buddy Holly providing guitar backing recorded Petty's beautiful 1957 release, "Moondreams". Holly also recorded the song, which was released posthumously. Unquestionably a steady performer, Petty was known more for the array of musicians who passed through his studio on their way to stardom: Roy Orbison, Buddy Knox, The String-A-Longs, Jimmy Gilmer and the Fireballs, Buddy Holly and The Crickets, and Waylon Jennings, to name a few. If Sam Phillips' Sun Studio had captured the leading southern rockabilly talent, Petty had done the same in the southwest.

It must be noted that Holly's later offerings, "Raining In My Heart" and "It Doesn't Matter Anymore", had also gone the way of big orchestras featuring a variety of stringed instruments. Recorded by Holly in 1958, the Dick Jacobs orchestrated songs became a two-sided hit for Holly shortly after his death. It was obvious that Snuff Garrett saw something special in Bobby's treatment of slower tempo material, although Bobby's first album, released in the fall of 1960, failed to chart.

Ironically, the album liner notes for *Bobby Vee Sings Your Favorites* are attributed to Norman Petty, owner of the Clovis recording studios. As mentioned, six of the rock and roll tracks recorded in Clovis were intended to be on the album, but were scrapped in favor of Los Angeles recorded ballads, of which Petty had no part.

By now, Liberty Records was approaching a quandary about Bobby's long-term value to the company. With sales of his previous singles dwindling and his debut album barely making a dent, Bobby had reached what may have been his last opportunity to record for a major record label. His most recent single, a cover of the old Ivory Joe Hunter hit "Since I Met You Baby" was floundering at #81 and, although it was an excellent rendition, it appeared to be suffering the same fate as his previous offering.

Then out of the blue a DJ at Pittsburg, PA radio station KQV flipped the record over and began playing the B-side, "Devil or Angel". That tune, also off the album, was a recycling of an old R&B song by The Clovers[37] and highly regarded by producer Snuff Garrett.

With Pittsburg leading the way, "Devil or Angel" began a steady rise up the pop charts and into the top ten in other major markets. By the end of the year and with generous airplay now available, it rose to #6 nationally.[38] The song also slipped into the

---

[37] The Clovers, a black R&B group, spawned several cover hits for white artists such as: "Lovey Dovey" by Buddy Knox; "Blue Velvet" Bobby Vinton, "From the Bottom of My Heart" the Diamonds; and "Love Potion Number 9" by the Searchers. "Devil or Angel" was a Clovers hit in 1956.

[38] In most instances, record chart placing's are based on Billboard Music Week's pop charts, generally known as the Hot 100 for singles and Top Album Sales for LPs. Billboard is the premier record industry

Top Twenty on Rhythm and Blues charts. Now, recognizing Bobby's immense potential, Liberty Records signed him to a five-year contract.

Liberty Records would not be disappointed, as Bobby's follow-up single "Rubber Ball"[39] equaled its predecessor's success by also rising to #6. It was his first of many offerings where Garrett overdubbed Bobby's voice, giving it a slight echo. This became much more common on future releases and was used successfully on many of Bobby's biggest hits. Cricket Jerry Allison was present and played on the record, something he did occasionally on some of Bobby's others songs. Interestingly, the Buddy Holly song "Everyday" was chosen as the record's B-side, providing a comparative look at how closely Bobby's interpretation and sound mimicked that of Holly's original.

With successive Top Ten smashes behind him, Bobby Vee's phenomenal career was well on its way.

Two Top Ten singles and a self-titled hit album, *Bobby Vee*, which peaked at #18 nationally, and an international star with hit records in other countries, the humble Bobby Velline was already the most famous Hi-Liner of Fargo Central High's Class of '61.

---

weekly. It tabulates record sales in many genres; reviews new song releases and publishes industry news.

[39] Interestingly, "Rubber Ball" was composed by popular 60's singer/songwriter Gene Pitney ("Town Without Pity", "The Man Who Shot Liberty Valance", "Only Love Can Break A Heart", "Twenty-four Hours From Tulsa", etc) and Aaron Schroeder (writer of many Elvis Presley hits: "Big Hunk of Love", "It's Now or Never", "Stuck on You", "Good Luck Charm" and many more.) Although Pitney co-wrote "Rubber Ball", contractual obligations prevented him from putting his own name on the song, so he used his mother's maiden name (Orlowski).

6

1960-62

During the early to mid 1960s, Bobby Vee consistently placed his records high in the charts, both nationally and overseas—"Rubber Ball" peaked at #4 on the UK charts and spent three weeks as Australia's number one record—however, he experienced a minor lull before hitting a spectacular year and a half stretch of Top Ten and Top Twenty hits.

The #6 USA charting of "Rubber Ball" would be followed by a moderate two-sided hit "Stayin' In"/"More Than I Can Say" at #33 and #61, respectively.[40]   It's difficult to understand why "Stayin' In" did not rise much higher. It was light and catchy, and similar to its predecessor, almost fitting into the novelty genre. It's believed in some circles that the song's mildly aggressive opening lines "I punched my buddy in the nose after lunch. Now I'm in trouble 'cause the dean saw the punch…"[41] may have stymied its radio airplay—and therefore limited its sales.

On the flip side of the disc it may be even more debatable why "More That I Can Say" did not break into the Top Ten. Leo Sayer's 1981 version of the Crickets Jerry Allison/Sonny Curtis song spent a remarkable five-weeks at #2 (UK's original Shadows also recorded a cover version). It seems the two sides of Bobby's record competed for chart placement, thus preventing either from becoming a much bigger hit.

But Bobby's April '61 "How Many Tears" charted even lower, at #63. This was certainly not the direction Liberty Records expected after Bobby's two highly successful Top Ten finishes earlier in the year. An album entitled, *Hit's of the Rockin' 50s,*

---

[40] Arguably, "More Than I Can Say", written by Crickets Sonny Curtis and Jerry Allison, was the stronger side. Leo Sayer's 1980 cover of the song spent five weeks at the #2 spot on Billboard's Hot 100 chart. The Crickets' original version topped out at #26 on the UK charts in 1960.

[41] Lyrics by John D. Loudermilk, Sony/ATV Music Publishing LLC.

with no singular Bobby Vee single to drive sales, would again put him back on the album charts. Adding to the album's sales appeal was the artfully done LP cover with Bobby dressed entirely in white, one leg draped casually over a rocking chair arm, in front of a stark black background. The fetching cover makes you want to pick it up and hear what's on the vinyl inside. The tracks consist of twelve recent pop/rock hits done in Bobby's inimitable style—a mix of ballads, mid-tempo tunes and flat-out rockers. Perhaps the most satisfying vocal is his reworking of The Five Keys' "Wisdom of A Fool". The album proved to be a successful endeavor, at it charted at #85, whereas its predecessor, *Bobby Vee With Strings and Things,* failed to chart.

Regardless of Bobby's delicate decline in popularity, the fact that he'd had a couple recent Top Ten sides, songwriters couldn't wait to get their new material to him.

A rapport had developed between Bobby and a pair of Brill Building[42] pop songwriters extraordinaire by the names of Carole King and Gerry Goffin[43]. King and Goffin were a hot commodity. The Shirelles had recently come off the #1 smash, "Will You Love Me Tomorrow", which was penned by the husband and wife team. Bobby himself had recorded the Goffin-King tune, "How Many Tears", although with far less success than The Shirelles' chart-topper.

While the young Fargo native was recording his *Bobby Vee With Strings and Things* album, Goffin and King flew out to visit him. During a break in the recording session, King sat down at a piano and sang two songs they'd just written. First was a

---

[42] New York City's Brill Building, located at 1619 Broadway, in Manhattan's Theater District, was a virtual assembly line song factory. Brill Building writers churned out hit after hit and many of the writers became immensely famous singers, as well. Among them were Neil Sedaka, Paul Anka, Carole King, Sonny Bono, Paul Simon and Neil Diamond. Brill also housed such famous writing teams as Doc Pomus and Mort Shuman, Jerry Leiber and Mike Stoller, Burt Bacharach and Hal David, and Barry Mann and Cynthia Weil—not to mention Gerry Goffin and Carole King. The list of successful writers, singers and hit songs credited to the Brill Building is immense!

[43] Goffin and King became two of the more prolific and successful writers working out of New York City's famous Brill Building. They also penned the number ones "The Loco-Motion" and "Go Away Little Girl", recorded by Little Eva and Steve Lawrence, respectively. Ironically, the latter song was offered to Bobby Vee, but he already had an abundance of good material. Steve Lawrence jumped at the chance to record it, taking it to #1 in late 1962. Donnie Osmond made it number one again, ten years later.

marvelous up-tempo number called "In My Baby's Eyes". It had single release written all over it. Next, however came the exclamation point to their cross-country visit, the remarkable "Take Good Care of My Baby". Bobby and Snuff couldn't wait to record it!

As one story goes, the Goffin-King team had written "Take Good Care of My Baby" for Dion, who had split from The Belmonts the year before to go solo. Snuff Garrett learned that Dion had in fact recorded the song, but did not intend to release it as a single. Dion soon released his self-composed (with Ernie Maresca) single "Runaround Sue", leaving the Goffin-King tune open for someone else to record.

Garrett decided to take the song anyway, but felt it needed an introductory (opening) verse. He and King set about to work on the song's opening narrative, coming up with the classic refrain, "My Tears are falling since you've taken her away[44]..." (Dion did in fact include "Take Good Care of My Baby" as an album track on his Runaround Sue LP.[45] Dion's album track version omits the spoken verse intro and is sung at a slightly faster tempo). Barely a week and a half later, Bobby Vee recorded and Liberty Records released what became his signature song.

It flew up the charts! Released in August, it reached the pinnacle of the singles chart the following month.

With "Take Good Care of My Baby" reaching number one, Bobby Vee had equaled his idol Buddy Holly's top of the chart successes. The album of the same name reached #91.

Vee's version soared up the charts, hitting the top spot on September 18, 1961. It remained at the top for three weeks, fending off Roy Orbison's classic "Crying" and Elvis Presley's "(Marie's the Name) His Latest Flame". "Crying" topped out at number two, thus preventing Roy Orbison from having two

---

[44] The opening refrain from the Goffin-King classic "Take Good Care of My Baby". Gerry Goffin and Carole King. Screen Gems Music, 1962.
[45] The Billboard Book of Number One Hits, pg 97, by Fred Bronson. Billboard Publications, Inc. 1985. ISBN 0-8230-7522-2

successive number one hits, Orbison's "Running Scared" having reached the top on June 5, 1961.

In another quirk of fate, Billboard's Top Five for the week of October 9, 1961 looked like this:[46] #1 Hit the Road Jack (Ray Charles); #2 Crying (Roy Orbison); #3 Take Good Care of My Baby (Bobby Vee); #4 Runaround Sue (Dion); and #5 Bristol Stomp (Dovells). By October 23, Dion's "Runaround Sue" pushed its way into the top spot and remained there for two weeks. Dion moved up to the top spot as Bobby slipped down.

The song began a series of several very successful singles released by Vee, many of which became two-sided hits. And, it solidified a long and fruitful relationship with Gerry Goffin and Carole King compositions.

But, like Dion had missed on releasing "Take Good Care of My Baby", Bobby and Snuff would soon miss on recording/releasing a surefire Goffin/King hit. The lyrics of a Goffin/King collaboration that would soon be an album track for Bobby went "I just let *My Golden Chance* go by..." However, "My Golden Chance" wasn't the song in question.

Goffin and King would present "Go Away Little Girl" to Bobby, but he already had a slew of good material waiting[47]. With little interest from Vee and his producer, the composers offered it to crooner Steve Lawrence ("Poinciana", "Pretty Blue Eyes", "Footsteps", and "Portrait of My Love"). After a successful stint with ABC Paramount, Lawrence had recently signed with the Columbia Records label. Lawrence went on to turn the song into a #1, achieving the top spot on January 21, 1963. (On September 11, 1971, Donnie Osmond's version would also achieve number one status. Both records would remain atop the chart for two weeks. If that wasn't enough, The Happenings made it a #12 hit in 1966).

---

[46] See record placement chart *The Top Five*, Week of October 23, 1961. The Billboard Book of Number One Hits, pg 97, by Fred Bronson. Billboard Publications, Inc. 1985. ISBN 0-8230-7522-2

[47] In a double twist of irony, Dion had turned down Goffin-King's "Take Good Care of My Baby", thus allowing Bobby Vee to turn it into a #1 chart topper, whereas Bobby turned down Goffin-King's "Go Away Little Girl", allowing Steve Lawrence to turn it into a #1!

Bobby's version would appear on his *The Night Has a Thousand Eyes* LP in 1963.

***

Providence would find Bobby, Snuff and the Crickets working together on the West Coast in 1961.

A superb Robert Velline (Bobby Vee) composition "I'm Feeling Better", with Bobby joining Jerry Allison on vocals, came out of the session. The song would be placed as the B-side of "He's Old Enough to Know Better", a novelty type track similar to Bobby's earlier "Stayin' In". Neither song on the disc created much attention, but the sessions began a creative partnership between Bobby and the Crickets, eventually culminating in a surprise hit album. More about that later...

The Crickets released several very good Liberty tracks during the next few years, but nothing became of the records stateside (although three records would find a degree of success in England). Later, an energetic reworking of "La Bamba" would make some local playlists in Michigan during the summer of '64, but that was pretty much the extent of it. Liberty certainly gave them an opportunity, but neither their singles nor albums made much of an impact.

***

Bobby's follow-up single to "Take Good Care of My Baby", "Run to Him" rose to #2 in December, being kept at bay only by The Tokens' "The Lion Sleeps Tonight", thus preventing the gifted Fargo kid from achieving successive chart-toppers.

In its own unique way, "Run to Him" has a similar sound to many of Roy Orbison's hits during this time—albeit more low-key, as very few could approach Orbison's dynamic vocal range and theatrics. "Run to Him" has a subdued, but rising crescendo that peaks with a dramatic, almost operatic ending. The song's success only helps solidify Bobby Vee as an ultra talented teen heartthrob. In an era when many artists covered proven hits on their albums, it poses the question why Bobby did not record some of Orbison's mega hits. He did, however, record an Orbison/Joe Melson composition entitled "Go On", as a minor track on his *Take Good Care of My Baby* album, "Lookin' For Love" on *Meets the Crickets* and Orbison's "Candy Man" on his *Meets the Ventures* LP. It leaves one to wonder how a Bobby Vee treatment of "Running Scared" or "It's Over" might have fared.

Having scored another huge hit, Bobby's first two singles for 1962, "Please Don't Ask About Barbara" and "Sharing You" by Goffin/King, would both reach number 15. It was certainly a commendable achievement, but not jaw dropping successful as his previous two releases.

In a bit of unusual trivia, "Please Don't Ask About Barbara" is one of the few Bobby Vee songs that Dick Clark declined to play on his daily teen dance show, *American Bandstand*. Clark was in the midst of a divorce. His estranged wife's name? You guessed it—Barbara.

In a time when many artists followed up a hit song with something closely identical, with "Please Don't Ask About Barbara", Bobby and Snuff again came up with a vibrant record that had no comparison to any of his previously released material. Whereas the beat to "Run to Him" loped along, "Barbara..." had a staccato rhythm. He gave both ballads beautiful treatments, but a person would never mistake one superb song for the other.

On the flip side, and there's no doubt it's a good backing track, "I Can't Say Goodbye", also eased into the Hot 100 at #92. That B-side was another Goffin-King gem. Teen hit maker, Bobby Rydell, released his version two-and-a-half years later. Rydell's version reached #94.

By then, as reflected on the back cover of his *Golden Greats* LP, Bobby had tabbed as the major influences in his career his personal manager Arnold Mills and record producer extraordinaire, Snuff Garrett. It's impossible to guess where Bobby's career might have led if someone other than Garrett had been at the controls. The two young men were in an extended phase of major hit records on the A-side and adequate minor to moderate hits on practically every B-side.

It's no wonder Bobby recognized his friend and producer Snuff Garrett in this admiring light.

So far, Liberty's attention was strictly on Bobby, so in March of '62, while Vee was away on the West Coast, the Strangers travelled to the Sara Sound Studio in Madison, WI and under the guidance of Jim Kirshteen's watchful eye cut ten songs in two days—mostly instrumentals. The taping went well and when Bobby got his hands on it, he took a copy of the tape to Liberty. Company execs were impressed and decided to release a few singles: "Toy Soldier" and "Card Shark" backed by "Mindreader".

In need of a keyboard player to overdub an organ part on "Toy Soldier", the Strangers brought in a talented young session musician named Leon Russell.[48] Much like former temporary keyboardist Zimmerman/Gunnn/Dylan, to say Russell had a "unique voice" would be understating the obvious. Liberty released "Toy Soldier" as a single, but it did not fare well. Already having a best-selling instrumental group in their stable, The Ventures, (recording for the Dolton label, a Liberty subsidiary), failure of "Toy Soldier" to gain serious interest undoubtedly doomed future Strangers releases.

Meanwhile, Bobby was continuing to find success both home and abroad—and in places other than primarily English speaking countries. In the USA, "Run To Him" was Billboard Magazine's #50 Top 100 Tune of 1962 and "Please Don't Ask About Barbara" was honored as Hong Kong's #12 song for the year. Billboard noted that with "the opening of the (city's) modern City Hall, Hong Kong played host to the London Philharmonic Orchestra, Frank Sinatra, ...Bobby Vee and Jo Ann Campbell."[49]

Next up, in April, Bobby went back to the Goffin-King well twice more for both sides: "Sharing You" backed with "In My Baby's Eyes". The A-side recaptured the beauty and heartbreak of "Run To Him", with a hint of Orbison-esque about it, but it only

---

[48] The longhaired Russell eventually found mid-70s fame as a solo artist with the songs "Tightrope" and "Lady Blue". His 1974 album *Carney* reached #2. Three years later, the Russell-penned "This Masquerade" earned a Grammy for Record of the Year for George Benson.

[49] *Billboard Music Week 1963 Who's Who in the World of Music.* December 29, 1962.

came to roost at #15. That high of a charting was a satisfactory achievement for many, but certainly not for someone who had reached the highest pinnacles of vinyl success.

Peculiarly, the flip side, "In My Baby's Eyes" is an energetic rocker with a spoken intro (a recurring theme with many of the Goffin-King compositions) that had enormous potential on its own, but unlike several of Bobby's less spirited B-sides that did chart, it received little noticeable airplay and failed to even crack the Top 100. Author's superfluous comment: *Although it failed to chart, it's always been a personal favorite!*

In June of that year Bobby recorded a gem of a song called "Tears Wash Her Away". With its unmistakable rolling opening beat, *dun dun-dun dun-dun dun-dun*, it's a combination of "Run To Him" and "Sharing You", but at a slightly faster cadence. It would have fit perfectly during that period—but maybe the question is *where would this recording have fit?* Bobby was in the middle of a year and a half run with singles charting number one, two and three with no A-side release dropping below number twenty. It may have come down to deciding whether to release "Tears…" or "Punish Her". I also see some similarities between the two. Perhaps it was a case of where he was so consistent with his hits, and the quality of his songs so high, that there was no place for it. That wouldn't explain why it wasn't used as an album track, however, or a later single release. It's a jewel of a song and it's impossible to understand how it did not get released in some form. Regardless, the song would not see the light of day until the *Rarities* CD was released in 2010. Note: *Some forty-plus years after many of the tracks were originally recorded, Bobby Vee historian and head of BV fan and collectors' clubs Bob Celli, obtained access to about 130 previously unissued tracks. Mr. Celli rough mixed the tracks and sent them to the Vee's RockHouse Studios where Bobby's son Jeff did the final mixing. From this project came the Rarities double CD.*[50]

---

[50] *Rare Rockin' Records* interview. Bob Celli Talks About Upcoming Bobby Vee Release. December 29, 2010.

As some artists were wont to do, select recordings were made primarily for overseas markets and not intended for a similar release within the USA. Dion would release certain tracks in Italy sung in Italian. Bobby would also record a handful of songs sung in Italian—"Run To Him"; "Charms"; "She's Sorry"; and "Come Back When You Grow Up". These songs are included on his The Singles Collection CD. Gene Pitney and Connie Francis would do likewise. UK star Cliff Richard recorded entire albums in Spanish, German, Italian, and French. However, obviously the easiest way to appease an overseas market's desire for new material was to release an English language record in an English speaking country. Roy Orbison did this in Australia, England and New Zealand.

Bobby Vee, in 1962 released "A Forever Kind of Love" from his *Bobby Vee Recording Session* disk, backed with "Remember Me, Huh", from the *Take Good Care of My Baby* LP. The former track was produced by Snuff Garrett and arranged by England's renowned Norrie Paramour. Paramour orchestrated most of Cliff Richard's highly successful catalog during this era.

The Goffin/King tune would become a #13 hit for Bobby in the UK, but Cliff Richard had recorded it a short time earlier. Cliff's version was not released as a single, perhaps because of the close timing to Bobby's venture—it was however, released by Richard's label on a 1964 Extended Play 45 titled *A Forever Kind Of Love*. Due to the success of Bobby's version in the UK, it provokes the question why Liberty didn't release it as a single stateside. Both versions are exemplary. Cliff Richard's version is done at a slightly faster tempo than Bobby's.[51]

It must be noted there were many similarities/parallels between America's Bobby Vee and England's Cliff Richard. Of course there's the irony of their early careers being fueled on the

---

[51] During the 1960s, Bobby Vee and Cliff Richard's styles and choices of material are quite similar. Both started their careers with faster, rock and roll oriented material. But as their popularity grew and they discovered greater success with milder material, that's what they gave their audiences. Both frequently recorded the same songs: "Theme For A Dream", "A Forever Kind of Love", "True Love Ways", It's fascinating that Paramor almost exclusively produced Cliff Richard's music throughout the early and mid 60s and was called upon to arrange Bobby Vee's "A Forever Kind of Love" for the UK market.

energy of stellar backing of two different bands named The Shadows. Both singers maintained impeccable images throughout their careers and occasionally covered one another's song, and Cliff's longtime music guru Norrie Paramor arranged and produced "A Forever Kind of Love" for both individuals. Furthermore, Cliff's manager Tito Burns served as Bobby's manager in England.

By July, Bobby was riding high in Great Britain. The UK's New Musical Express had him at #7 in its World's Most Outstanding Singer poll[52] for the first half of the year. He's entrenched in the elite company of Cliff Richard, Elvis Presley, The Shadows (UK), and the Everly Brothers.

At the height of Bobby's popularity, a TV special entitled *The Idol – The Story of Bobby Vee* was proposed. It was intended to document his rise in stardom and chronicle his career. The following songs were to be aired in the special: "Walkin' With My Angel", "Suzie Baby", "Keep A Knocking", "The Idol" and "You Won't Forget Me". A theme song was chosen and given to Bobby, but before he could record it, United Air Lines Pilot Jack Lewis, the writer, pulled the song and gave it to Ricky Nelson. The documentary was never aired.

Liberty Records pretty much stuck to a four singles per year agenda for Bobby. By the end of summer, it was time for a new record. But the late summer release for '62, "Punish Her" fell a little further from the top, reaching only #20. Since his #1 and #2 punch and counter punch of "Take Good Care of My Baby" and "Run To Him", Bobby's singles had steadily declined, dropping to #15, #15 and now #20. Many artists would consider these chartings a major success, but for Bobby Vee and Tommy Garrett, they weren't up to Snuff (pun intended!)

"Punish Her" had all the ingredients for a hit record—spoken intro, catchy lyrics and medium tempo beat—but it didn't catch fire as many of his previous records had done.

---

[52] The New Musical Express's World's Most Outstanding Singer chart is determined by awarding 30 points for each week at number 1, down to 1 point for each week at number 30.

Perhaps more importantly than Bobby Vee's continued slow slide down the top singles charts, the flip side of "Punish Her" found him being backed by The Crickets.[53] Bobby and original Cricket drummer Jerry Allison were staying in the same apartment building in L.A. and wanted to do a rock album, although Liberty wanted him to stick with the contemporary sound that was making him hits and the company money. The boys ultimately prevailed and from that came one of Bobby's finest LPs.   The B-side tune, "Someday (When I'm Gone From You)" showcased Bobby in one of his most rousing Liberty performances to date. It was pure rock and roll and easily matched up with anything on the charts at the time. Just give a quick listen to the jangling lead guitar, rolling drums, Bobby's double-tracked Holly-like vocal and the superb background echo each time he sings the word "someday" and tell me your foot doesn't begin stomping out the marvelous beat. It was another great Vee B-side, but it would barely squeak in at #99. Regardless of its scanty chart placing, it would find its way onto perhaps Bobby's very best and most complete R&R album, *Bobby Vee Meets the Crickets*.

The record company, like many of the fans, had come to reward pop songs and strings more than down to earth rock and roll.   The LP, recorded the year before, was conceived with specific guidelines in mind, but the recording was not going according to plan so Vee and the Crickets decided to scrap that idea and simply play songs they liked. That spontaneity is how "Little Queenie" and other R&R classics made it onto the recording—and perhaps that's why the album has such a fresh

---

[53] In 1961 the Crickets signed with Liberty Records and scored a UK Top Five single with the Goffin/King tune "Don't Ever Change". The song was offered to Bobby, but he declined and gave it to The Crickets. The record did little stateside, but reached Top 5 in England. The then unknown voice of Glen Campbell harmonized with the group on the record's flip side, "I'm Not A Bad Guy". (Campbell appeared often as a session musician/vocalist, backing an array of artists like Elvis Presley, Ricky Nelson, the Champs, and Jan and Dean. He also had a brief association with the Beach Boys filling in for Brian Wilson). In addition to their collaborative LP with Vee, The Crickets released two albums *Something Old, Something New, Something Blue, Something Else(1963)* and *California Sun (1964)* on the Liberty label. Bobby Vee provided backup vocals on some of the Liberty tracks.

sound. Unlike Bobby's earlier albums that favored lush ballads or catchy pop, *Meets the Crickets* simply rocks out.

Among the stellar tracks, "Peggy Sue" and "Well, All Right" are Holly throwbacks. "Lucille" and Bobby Troup's "The Girl Can't Help It" pay homage to Little Richard. "Sweet Little Sixteen" and "Little Queenie" acknowledge the great Chuck Berry. But arguably the best track is "When You're in Love", written by Crickets Jerry Allison and Sonny Curtis. Allison's frenetic working of the drums and clanging cymbals are beyond perfect. This is as close to a Holly reincarnation as you will ever hear.

However, the folks at Liberty were uninspired and decided to release an album that was more in line with their usual product, so they released both *A Bobby Vee Recording Session* AND *Bobby Vee Meets the Crickets* at the same time. This was an almost unheard of practice to have competing LPs released simultaneously. *A Bobby Vee Recording Session* certainly had high sales potential containing hit singles "Sharing You" and "Please Don't Ask About Barbara", plus "In My Baby's Eyes" and a couple singles contenders (had they been released as such) "My Golden Chance" and another fine Crickets' composition, "Teardrops Fall Like Rain".[54]

Perhaps surprisingly, and showing that corporate executives didn't quite have it right, *A Bobby Vee Recording Session* charted at a very strong #121 in the USA, but *Bobby Vee Meets the Crickets* rose all the way to #42. The public knew what it wanted. One wonders how much higher the LP might have gone had Liberty not cluttered the closet with the two simultaneous releases and had they devoted a solid effort to promote it.

---

[54] "Teardrops Fall Like Rain" composed by T. Lesslie, J. Allison and G. Hardin, Cricket Music-Saima Music, BMI. The Crickets released their version in January 1963, as a B-side. The A-side for the record was another Cricket composition, "My Little Girl" by Sonny Curtis. They're two excellent tracks that got lost among all the rest of the vinyl being released at the time. The best that "My Little Girl" could achieve was one week on the Bubbling Under chart at #134. The song is credited to Cricket Music-Saima Music, which indicates a strong likelihood that Bobby Vee had more than a passing interest in the song. Other self-penned songs in his catalog are published by Saima Music; Saima being Bobby's mother's name.

Even with these drawbacks, *Meets the Crickets* did extremely well. It would soar even higher in the UK, topping out at a remarkable #3!

But, next up, "The Night Has a Thousand Eyes" coming at the end of the year as it did, did little to bolster Bobby's yearend chart positioning. One is hard pressed to even find the slightest mention of his name in Billboard Music Week's 1963 *Who's Who in the World of Music*. Presley, Boone, Dion, Vinton, Cliff Richard are there, as are Del Shannon, Gene Pitney, Anka, Rydell and Brian Hyland, but surprisingly no Bobby Vee! The young man who had scored a number one and a number two hit the year before, as brilliant as those songs were, could only muster two records at number 15.

***

The end of the year found Liberty releasing the LP *Merry Christmas From Bobby Vee*. Along with the usual Christmas fare would be two magnificent original surprises: "A Not So Merry Christmas" and "My Christmas Love".

Oddly, Liberty decided to forego releasing Bobby's "A Not So Merry Christmas" as a seasonal single. It was a sure-fire hit and corporate execs flat missed it. Unlike the song's title, the year would end on a very merry note. The Christmas album finished out the successful year at #136.

The Music of Bobby Vee

Robert Reynolds

7

1963-64

Although RCA, Columbia, Capital, Mercury, Decca and MGM were the primary power players in the record industry, with the Motown trifecta of Tamla, Motown, and Gordy on their way up, the Liberty conglomerate was no shrinking violet. Pick any Billboard Hot 100 chart during the period and you would be hard pressed not to find a slew of Liberty and its affiliates' records scattered about the charts. In fact, an article in Billboard Music Week, June 30, 1962, advised: *Liberty Records tied RCA Victor for first place in the singles race for the first six months of 1962 by placing nine records in the Top 50 of BMW's "Hot 100", the same number as Victor.*[55]

Liberty Records had a formidable roster of capable artists when 1963 rolled in—Johnny Burnette, Gene McDaniels, Billy Ward, Julie London, Martin Denny, Jan and Dean, Timi Yuro, Vikki Carr, even aging western character actor Walter Brennan had scored a #5 with the maudlin "Old Rivers" the year before. As might be suspected, Snuff Garrett produced the Brennan hit. Liberty subsidiary labels like Imperial had Fats Domino, Rick(y) Nelson, drummer Sandy Nelson, Jackie DeShannon, Mel Carter, Santo and Johnny, and would soon sign Johnny Rivers. Dolton Records was loaded with The Ventures, The Fleetwoods and Vic Dana.

Many of the label's album insert sleeves announced Liberty's "Sound of the 'Sixties!" and it's no wonder. Certainly in part what gave Liberty records a cohesive sound, be it rockabilly extraordinaire Johnny Burnette, soulful Gene McDaniels, teen crooner Bobby Vee or countrified Walter Brennan, the ultra

---

[55] *Liberty Ties Victor For Singles Lead (Mercury, Decca 45 Runners Up),* Billboard Music Week (page 6), June 30, 1962, by Bob Rolontz.

smooth Johnny Mann Singers[56] often provided the background vocals regardless of who the artist was.

Similarly, the great Ernie Freeman was responsible for much of the arranging and orchestral conducting. Freeman's orchestra itself had hit pay dirt with a #4 rendition of the Glenn Miller classic, "In the Mood", garnering a gold record in 1959 on the Rendezvous label. It was common to find the names Mann and Freeman on countless Liberty disks. This was especially true about Bobby Vee's recordings.

After reaching the top of the charts with a #1, followed by a #2 record, Bobby's chart success had been on the wane. It wasn't a huge drop off, but for a star of his magnitude his next three singles would top out no higher than #20. Not bad for most, but disappointing for someone who had reached the very top.

But, Liberty execs needed not to worry. With Freeman conducting and the Mann Singers behind him, Bobby Vee would again reach lofty chart success with his upbeat December '62 release, "The Night Has a Thousand Eyes". The Benjamin Weisman, Dorthy Wayne and Marilyn Garrett tune would rocket up the charts and reach #3 in the USA and in the UK. The song's frantic up-tempo deviated greatly from his recent ballads and was a pure out rocker that showed what Bobby could do with faster (and adequate) material—and that his fans wanted it. The immense success of "The Night Has a Thousand Eyes" was an unexpected surprise.

The giant hit came at a time when many studios were recording in live time. In fact, Bobby and Snuff would record live until 1964. With the machines rolling, the band would begin and the singers jump in. If a take went bad or was not satisfactory, the vocalists and musicians would run through the entire song again, recording as many takes as needed until they felt they had it right. Regarding "The Night Has a Thousand Eyes", Bobby, Ernie

---

[56] The Johnny Mann Singers, generally three men and three women, sang backup on most of Bobby Vee's records. The group was used extensively with many other Liberty artists, including Johnny Burnette, Walter Brennan, Eddie Cochran, The Crickets and many others. The Johnny Mann Singers also recorded roughly three-dozen of their own albums.

Freeman's Orchestra and the Mann Singers took all of twelve minutes to record one of his biggest hits.

Unfortunately for Bobby and crew at Liberty, it would be his last top five hit for the next 4½ years.

Backed, as he generally was by the Johnny Mann Singers and Ernie Freeman's exceptional arrangement, Bobby's follow-up single, "Charms", reached #5 on the Adult Contemporary Chart, but only climbed to #13 on the Billboard Hot 100. For someone of lesser musical stature, it would have been considered a huge success. If there was any consolation, perhaps it was that the flip side, "Bobby Tomorrow" charted at #21 in the UK. "Charms" a catchy ditty in the vein of Cliff Richard's 1960 UK single "Theme For a Dream",[57] would be Bobby's last Top Twenty offering for this era.

A mid '63 LP release titled *Bobby Vee Meets the Ventures* was his highest charting album since *Golden Greats*. The disk tried to recapture the chemistry of his *Meets the Crickets* LP a year before, but it was less intimate and the selected tracks seemed less cohesive than those on the *Crickets'* LP. Arguably the best tracks were "Walk Right Back" and Ray Sharpe's "Linda Lou(sic)". Two tracks were Ventures' instrumentals, apparently intended to showcase their superb guitar work unhindered by vocals. Whereas *Meets the Crickets* came across like a relaxed, spontaneous project, at times *Meets the Ventures* seems strained. From an artistic standpoint, the continuation of collaborative albums did not fare well in this instance, although the record reached #91. From that aspect I'm sure that Liberty exec were pleased.

Also released that year was *I Remember Buddy Holly*, a tribute LP featuring eleven Holly classics and a song entitled "Buddy's Song". Its lyrics were primarily made up of Holly song

---

[57] Bobby Vee had covered Richard's "Theme For A Dream" on his *The Night Has A Thousand Eyes* LP. It was one of several excellent songs on the album, including Jackie DeShannon's "You Won't Forget Me" and covers of Steve Lawrence's "Go Away Little Girl", Carole King's "It Might As Well Rain Until September" (both of these Goffin-King penned songs were offered to Bobby the same time as "Take Good Care of My Baby", but Bobby had an abundance of good music so he turned them down. Here, we get to hear the superb treatments he gave them.)

titles and snippets of lyrics from the various songs. Although someone else obviously put it together, songwriting credits are listed as Buddy Holly. The album is loaded with exceptional Buddy Holly covers and is overwhelmingly superior to his *Meets the Ventures* LP, but unfortunately it failed to chart.

Vee's interpretation of "Raining In My Heart", "It Doesn't Matter Anymore", "Think It Over" and "Maybe Baby" are pure delight. It's hard to imagine any other singer from that era covering the Holly material with such passion and perfection. Snuff Garrett could easily have led Bobby down the same path as Buddy and achieved some degree of success, but he wisely did not. Bobby's talent went far beyond imitating another artist.

Although four years had passed since the tragic plane crash in an Iowa cornfield, perhaps the album came too soon after Holly's demise. Several more years would pass before the memory of Buddy Holly really caught hold and people truly began to appreciate Holly's genius.

Even though Liberty had released three Vee albums that year, they weren't finished yet.

Several tracks were recorded for a planned 1963 LP entitled *The Wonderful World of Bobby Vee*,[58] but a corporate decision scrapped the project. Those tracks would remain unreleased until a British compact disc of the album was released in 2001.

Perhaps based on the admirable ranking of "Charms" in the Adult Contemporary charts, some of Bobby's next singles appear to have targeted toward a more mature audience (*Note: this is purely conjecture, however*). "Be True To Yourself", the beautiful "Never Love A Robin", and the underappreciated "Yesterday and You (Armen's Theme)" surely seem to be an attempt to move away from teen themed songs.

---

[58] Liberty Records had planned a series of *Wonderful World Of....* Albums, recognizing many of their star talents, such as Julie London, Gene McDaniels, Walter Brennan, and of course Bobby Vee. The first three of these LPs were released with only moderate success and Liberty shut down the project. The aborted Bobby Vee album was scheduled as the fourth in the series. It finally saw light as a UK released compact disc in 2001.

Bobby later remarked about "Be True To Yourself", "It was really on the edge of my range and it was all I could do to sing the song. Their (Burt Bacharach/Hal David) songs were like that... Hal David is still one of my favorite lyricists."[59]

Liberty wasn't the only label experimenting with moving its R&R and teen-oriented singers into a more adult direction. Columbia, with it's first Dion LP, *Ruby Baby*, along with a handful of rock songs, included middle of the road chestnuts "You're Nobody 'til Somebody Loves You", "You Made Me Love You (I Didn't Want to Do It)", "Fever" and a surprising rendition of Al Jolson's "My Mammy!" Rick(y) Nelson soon released "Fools Rush In" and followed it up with "For You" and "The Very Thought of You". Pat Boone had been courting a more mature audience years before with albums titled *Pat Sings Irving Berlin, Stardust, Tenderly* and *Moonglow* in 1958-60. And overseas, England's "Elvis", Cliff Richard, had peppered his LPs with old standards like "As Time Goes By", "That's My Desire", "The Touch of Your Lips", "Almost Like Being in Love", and "Sentimental Journey". His 1963 single "It's All In the Game" became a Top 25 hit in the USA. Many record companies still believed that rock and roll was a passing whim and they were looking for the next Sinatra, Dean Martin or Vaughn Monroe.

In fact, another Bobby had transitioned from rock and roller quite successfully. Waldon Robert Cassotto, 5-years Vee's senior, had evolved quite profitably into Bobby Darin, growing from novelty songs like "Splish Splash" (#3), "Queen of the Hop" (#9) and "Plain Jane" (#38) to the first-rate "Dream Lover" (#2) and then the Showbiz tune, "Mack the Knife" from the German play, *The Threepenny Opera*. Darin's giant hit "Mack..." spent nine weeks at the number one spot in late 1959 and many of his singles from that time on would be standards such as "Beyond the Sea", "Clementine", "Lazy River" and "Nature Boy". "Mack the Knife" would go on to capture a Grammy for Record of the Year in 1960.

---

[59] Quote extracted from Serene Dominic's *Song By Song: The ultimate Burt Bacharach reference for fans, serious collectors, and music critics.*

Darin and Pat Boone were two of the most successful teen idols to make the leap to adult fare.

Vee's rendition of "Yesterday and You" proved that he certainly could perform adult oriented material, even though the song's chart showing might not as yet reflect it.

Several superb tracks would come out since his last notable hit, "Charms", but none of them charted high, with most lingering in the middle to lower end of the Hot 100.

His exceptional "Yesterday and You" was a retitled cover of the Ross Bagdasarian[60] tune "Armen's Theme". It's a relaxed, catchy song reminiscent of Elvis Presley's "It's Now or Never". It's one of those melodies that stick in your head and you find yourself singing along without any thought of it. Retitled for Bobby as "Yesterday and You", it rose to #55. It deserved to go much higher. Had it been recorded by crooners Sinatra, Vic Dana, or Andy Williams, it surely would have gotten far more airplay in the Adult Contemporary market.

Overseas, Bobby again made an early showing in the New Musical Express chart coming in at #9 for the first quarter. But by the end of the year Cliff Richard would be crowned the World's Most Outstanding Singer, with Elvis Presley following as runner-up.

Bobby's life was moving at a rapid pace. A year earlier on the back cover of his *Golden Greats* album, Liberty liner notes had listed "Facts About Bobby" thus: "Likes: Girls" and "Weakness: Pretty girls." Most assuredly this was a Liberty marketing ploy meant to tweak the attention of teenage lasses, as he was then, and always, singularly committed to his long time sweetheart, Karen Bergan. By the time he and the lovely Karen married on December 28, 1963[61] at the Holy Rosary Church in her hometown of Detroit Lakes, Bobby already had 11 Top 40 hits.

[60] Bagdasarian, aka David Seville, among other things was a musician, actor, and record producer, perhaps most famous for creating the highly successful novelty act (records, TV show, movies) Alvin and the Chipmunks, and for the 1960 novelty hit "Witch Doctor".

[61] Take Good Care of My Baby: Bobby Vee and his wife celebrate 50 years; by Jon Bream, Star Tribune, April 13, 2014

With his marriage, studio time and touring, there was little time for the young man to relax. The follow-up to "Yesterday and You", "Stranger In Your Arms" is an extremely well produced, splendidly vocalized song that ranks high among Bobby's best. It might have fared better had it come out soon after "The Night Has A Thousand Eyes", as it carried an up-tempo beat and a memorable storyline about feeling left out, *à la* an outsider having impeded their romance. It's undoubtedly one of Bobby Vee's overlooked gems. Dwindling airplay doomed it to a mere #83 standing.

But there would be no rest.

The United Kingdom having proven to be a major market, Bobby boarded a plane for a flight across the Atlantic. Nightly shows, promotional visits and rehearsals kept him on the run.

Guitar based groups had begun to dominate the airwaves. In many ways the sound and energy were reminiscent of early American rock and roll; Eddie Cochran, Gene Vincent, Holly and early Presley. In fact, many of the "new" songs were covers of early rock and roll and rhythm and blues. The music of Muddy Waters, Willie Dixon, Lightnin' Hopkins and other underappreciated Black R&B musicians was being "discovered" and finding its way onto vinyl via the British groups.

The Beatles, Rolling Stones, Dave Clark Five, Searchers, Fourmost, Animals, Billy J. Kramer and the Dakotas, Herman's Hermits, Swinging Bluejeans, Nashville Teens, The Who, The Zombies, Them, The Yardbirds Manfred Mann, Moody Blues, Ian Whitcomb, Gerry and the Pacemakers, Peter and Gordon, and the Hollies were among many British bands swarming the airwaves.

While touring Northern England, a member of the Merseybeats introduced Bobby to the new British sound—ironically, many of the new British groups were covering U.S. stalwarts, Carl Perkins, Little Richard, and of course, Holly. Even more surprising, the Beatles had covered "Take Good Care of My Baby" for their January '62 Decca Records audition.

After returning back home and on tour in the Northwest with Snuff Garrett, someone played the Beatles' "Love Me Do" for them. It sounded very much like The Crickets and Garrett wanted to buy the rights for release in America, but the $25,000 asking price was too high.

Years later, Bobby would say, "We could tell that they (Beatles) were going to be popular and I started to learn their tunes. I also wrote six or seven tunes such as 'She's Sorry' in that fashion. It was done with the kindest of intentions, a proclamation that there was this new sound in England. It never entered my mind that I was ripping them off, although it may look like that now." [62]

Bobby needed not to worry about that because it was an erroneous perception. If we are to apply that belief to his, or any other American artist's perceived attempt to copy the British sound, we must conclude the same thing about the British artists who covered Perkins, Chuck Berry and many others (the Beatles— "Match Box"; "Honey Don't"; "Everybody's Trying to Be My Baby"; "Blue Suede Shoes"; "Roll Over Beethoven"; "Johnny B. Goode"; "Memphis, Tennessee"; "Dizzy Miss Lizzy"; "Slow Down"; and on it goes). The Rolling Stones would be guilty of covering to death Muddy Waters, Chuck Berry and Otis Redding. Two of the Searchers most popular numbers were reworking's of Jackie DeShannon's "Needles and Pins" and "When You Walk In the Room". It's erroneous to assume one thing unless we assume the other.

With his creative juices now flowing, Bobby set about writing and interpreting his own brand of British music—the result, a catchy ditty called "I'll Make You Mine"—complete with Beatlesque "oohs" and exaggerated "yeahs" emitting from the background. Upon hearing his new Beatles inspired single, some disc jockeys good-naturedly took to announcing the song's artist as "Bobby Veetle".

---

[62] Extracted from Mersey Beat article, by Spencer Leigh May 29, 2013 - http://www.spencerleigh.co.uk/tag/merseybeat/

From within the recording studio soon came his British influenced *New Sound From England* LP in mid '64. It worked to some extent as it modestly charted at #146 on the album charts. Lennon-McCartney's "She Loves You" and "From Me To You" are among the tracks as are four Bobby Vee composed songs. Bobby wasn't the first American artist to record Beatles' tracks. Del Shannon had released his single "From Me To You" the year before, charting in at #77. And Gene Pitney recorded and released as a single the Mick Jagger/Keith Richards tune "That Girl Belongs to Yesterday", #49.

The "She Loves You" sounding "I'll Make You Mine" backed by "She's Sorry" was his highest charting single in the past year coming in at #52. That was 31 points higher than his previous single "Stranger In Your Arms", which from a personal standpoint I feel is the stronger offering. "I'll Make You Mine" failed to chart in England, however—the British apparently were not overwhelmed at his attempt to encroach on their musical turf. Both sides of that release are listed as Bobby Vee with the Eligibles.[63] During that same year while again touring the British Isles, Bobby and the Beatles would meet.

"I'll Make You Mine's" successor "Hickory, Dick and Dock" equaled the former's chart showing, but it did not hold the excitement of Bobby's previous work. In fact, there was little deejay excitement in any of the last several sides released during 1964.

Liberty closed out the year with the release of *30 Big Hits of the 60's*. It was an album entirely of covers of other artist's hit songs. Not a single original Bobby Vee tune appeared on the disc. It failed to chart and began a three-year period of similarly doomed albums.

Several factors may have accounted for Bobby's sluggish chart performance during this period. It's well documented that

[63] Bobby Vee's British Invasion influenced single "I'll Make You Mine" b/w "She's Sorry" reflect the artist(s) as Bobby Vee and the Eligibles. Group endeavors were extremely popular during this period and perhaps adding The Eligibles' name to the record was an attempt to capture the British Invasion sound/audience. The Eligibles may have been pop/country star Sonny James' backup group.

the influx of British performers onto the American music scene had inflicted damage to many of our top stars. Except for Elvis Presley's gospel hymn, "Crying In the Chapel" even he was hard pressed to find the Top Ten. Pat Boone had practically disappeared from the singles' charts—although his studio albums featuring lush standards continued to do well. Dion took to recording old blues covers and then moved toward folk-rock, but with minimal success. Jackie Wilson had not had a top hit since 1963's dance number "Baby Workout". Del Shannon's records were hit and miss. Connie Francis was all but forgotten, as was Rick(y) Nelson. The once routine hits of Frankie Avalon, Fabian, Freddy Cannon, Paul Anka and Bobby Rydell had dried up.

Some of these artists would again strike pay dirt years on. Dion's "Abraham, Martin and John" would reach #4 in 1968. Rick Nelson struck gold in '72 with his #6 "Garden Party". Jackie Wilson caught lightning in both '66 and '67 with #11 "Whispers" and #6 "Higher and Higher". Seemingly eons later, Roy Orbison hit #9 with "You Got It" in 1989. But during 1964, these past superstars were little more than footnotes in American music history.

Gene Pitney, the Four Seasons and the Beach Boys seemed to be holding their own in the onrushing wave of Brits, but few others. The Supremes, Marvin Gaye, The Miracles, The Temptations, Four Tops and the rest of the Motown stable were chugging right along, churning out hits one after the other. But, like the overseas movement, the music coming out of Detroit was a newer, fresher sound, too.

Perhaps Bobby's surefire string of hits had simply run its course. Everyone's star eventually diminishes and his or her popularity ends. It seemed that Bobby Vee's incredible run was nearing that end.

Bobby's music wasn't languishing from lack of trying. "Ev'ry Little Bit Hurts" has that stop and go cadence similar to 1962's "Anonymous Phone Call" (B-side for "The Night Has A Thousand Eyes"). The flip side, "Pretend You Don't See Her" is a lush, romantic ballad, somewhat akin to an Andy Williams presentation. The great Jerry Vale took it to #52 in 1957. If Liberty still intended to turn Bobby into a crooner, now would have been the ideal time. With this melody and "Yesterday and You" leading the way with old standards, it might have made for an interesting album and coaxed a more mature audience into the Vee fold—but little happened with the single.

Next up, the steady feel-good orchestration of "Cross My Heart" is reminiscent of Detroit group The Reflections' #6 blue-eyed soul masterpiece, "Romeo and Juliet" and its successor "Keep On Trying" employs a bass/piano intro common to many of the soulful Motown recordings coming out of Detroit's West Grand Boulevard neighborhood studio. But, nothing seemed to work. As good as many of his songs were he was mired in mediocre chartings. Something had to change.

So began a period of each new release being recorded under the guidance of a different producer. Gone were the days of Bobby Vee and Snuff Garrett racking up hits. The label seemed stymied at finding a project and a producer who could put Bobby Vee back on top.

During the year, Liberty released an album that even Bobby was disappointed with, the faux live album, *Live, On Tour.* Although there are some nice tracks, the "canned" applause does not work well—as is the case with most fake "live" albums, regardless of whom the artist is. It failed to chart.

Finally in late 1965 the extraordinary "Run Like the Devil" emerged. The Dave Pell production had all the ingredients to become a monster hit—great melody, appealing lyrics, and a crescendo building theme. It was the incomparable Bobby Vee sound from earlier years. Why this song failed to become a hit is mindboggling. The mediocre showings of the past year's singles had taken their toll and the song received virtually no airplay. "Run Like the Devil" would not reach the Top 100, languishing at a dismal #124. Bafflingly, it did not even find its way onto an album for almost three years when a different mix finally surfaced on 1968's *Do What You Gotta Do* LP.

1965 would end with Bobby reworking an old Marty Robbins hit, "The Story of My Life", under the production of Joe Saraceno. It's an adequate rendering, if one is looking for adequacy, but it does not set itself apart from the many other great tunes vying for radio time. Perhaps Bobby was paying homage to Robbins. As mentioned, it was a nice version, but did it not set itself apart from the pack.

Bobby: "...(My) brother Bill was five years older than me, but he would take me to the shows. I saw a lot of people — never saw Hank Williams, but I saw Johnny Cash a couple of times, Marty Robbins a few times, Jimmy Newman, Ernest Tubb and that's the stuff I loved. I didn't get to see Johnny Horton, but he was another one of my favorites. That was the rockin' part of country that really appealed to me."[64]

The record's flip side, the Van Dyke Parks/Bobby Vee penned "High Coin" was fresher and more exhilarating than "The Story of My Life".

Glen Campbell's 1967 "Gentle On My Mind" and Bobby Goldsboro's 1968 "The Straight Life", both later hits for their respective artists, seem similar in theme and arrangement to "High Coin". It appears Bobby was ahead of the time with this surprisingly delightful, but short-lived recording.

Relegated to the B-side, "High Coin" garnered little interest as it, too, failed to chart.

By comparing record label numbers, on the surface it seems that Liberty released three Bobby Vee sides within a relatively short period—Liberty 55828, Liberty 55843 ("Story of My Life/High Coin") and Liberty 55854. It's perplexing why Liberty did this, because it hardly gave the record a chance to catch on.

Perhaps more of a surprise, and mystery, was the February '66 release of "A Girl I Used to Know" b/w "Gone". These

---

[64] Quote from *I Wouldn't Change A Thing*. Goldmine Magazine Interview. Craig Moore. April 30, 2009.

undeniably country songs appear to have been recorded in the early 60's, with the latter being pulled off his 1960 album *Bobby Vee Sings Your Favorites*. The former is a cover of the George Jones hit from 1962 and the latter a 1957 hit for Ferlin Husky. It's difficult to understand what Liberty was thinking unless with their floundering attempts to find a hit for him, they lobbed out this release hoping the country market might be interested. The A-side managed a paltry showing at #133 on the Bubbling Under chart, but basically, the record went nowhere. It was the only attempt to go country, although in a few years Bobby's music took a distinctly folk direction, often with a country flair.

1966 would see the release of another *30 Big Hits of the 60's* album, volume two. Like the first album, it showcased Bobby's ability to sing almost any style of song with exceptional results. Many of the songs were medleys, combining two into one. It was a nice album, but with no individual Bobby Vee tracks, it appeared that Liberty was again only going through the motion. I'm assuming the company had a contractual commitment they were simply fulfilling.

Here I'll digress from the music for a moment and discuss the aesthetic aspect of Bobby's albums during this period. Bobby's first several album covers were very well done and add considerable interest to the disc and material inside. How can a person not want to inspect the contents of *A Bobby Vee Recording Session* just from seeing the cool cover photo of Bobby with tie loosened and standing before a mic? Or how about the great cover for *Sings Hits of the Rockin' '50's*? Some LP covers are just plain appealing—Dion's *Runaround Sue* and *Alone With Dion*; Roy Orbison's *Lonely and Blue*; Del Shannon's *Little Town Flirt*; Jackie Wilson's *So Much*; John Stewart's *California Bloodlines*...

However, the covers for Bobby's two *30 Big Hits of the 60's* albums are identical. They use the same photo of Bobby and an identical green background. The only differences are the print formats and background colors behind the song listings. The original LP has a white background behind the track list while the background for *Volume Two* is black. The LP cover for the first volume is quite nice, but it's inexcusable of Liberty to put so little effort into the second cover. Evidently the corporate accountants were counting pennies and it was cheaper to reuse the same cover rather than spend money on a photo shoot.

This being said, Liberty wasn't the only company to shortchange the covers of some of their biggest moneymakers. The ultra plain and unimaginative LP jackets for Laurie Records' *Dion Sings His Greatest Hits* and *More of Dion's Greatest Hits* are almost embarrassing. Monument Records' stark white cover for *The All-time Greatest Hits of Roy Orbison* did not provide a photo of the artist on the front of the jacket. For that matter many of his 45-rpm picture sleeves were bland and without photo. At least Bobby's photo was featured on the covers of the two albums, even though it was the same photo.

This would not be the only time Liberty resorted to similar tactics as we will later see with his two 1968 albums.

8

A CAREER REKINDLED (1965-1970)

As the mid 60s raced along with Bobby's records routinely suffering in the depths of the charts, in came Dallas Smith to produce much of Bobby's new music (although an occasional Garrett produced track would emerge). Smith had produced albums for garage rock bands The Gants ("Roadrunner"), Hourglass (forerunner to the Allman Brothers Band), and Del Shannon, who had recently come into the Liberty fold. Shannon, too, had fallen on hard times and was looking for a hit record. His last hit was early '65's "Stranger In Town", which had come in at #30. Now with Liberty, he was hoping for resurgence to his career.

Although Bobby's career was also in a holding pattern, he continued to release singles and albums with almost the same regularity as before. The problem was that his efforts languished in the lower half of the charts.

August, October and November of '65 would find him in the studio and behind the mic searching for that illusive hit.

Regardless of their commitment to striking it big again, Bobby's recording of the David Gates composed "You'll Be Needing Me Baby" slipped away unnoticed and was locked away in Liberty's vaults for the next thirty-five years. It's one of those exceptional songs that Bobby had in his grasp, but for some reason it was not released commercially. Nino Tempo and April Stevens would release it as a single in '67.

Incidentally, Gates went on to front the 70's soft rock band Bread.

About April '66, Liberty issued Bobby's cover of the splendid "Butterfly" by Barry and the Tamerlanes. Note: *This is not the same "Butterfly" that Bobby recorded with the Shadows years before. These are two distinctly different songs.* Snuff Garrett and Leon Russell produced the song. (Since Dallas Smith had taken the production reins over Bobby's music, it's possible Snuff Garrett produced "Butterfly" earlier and the song only now saw the light of day, but I cannot confirm this). As expected, Bobby performs a very commendable adaptation of the of the Barry DeVorzon/Don Crawford original. It was released with "Save A Love" (a mediocre tune at best) as its B-side, but quickly withdrawn.

"Save A Love" would then be re-released as the B-side to the Dallas Smith produced "Look At Me Girl". Both "Butterfly" b/w "Save A Love" and "Look At Me Girl" b/w "Save A Love" reflect the same record release number, F-55877. It's unclear why Liberty pulled "Butterfly" and why they reissued the same record release number. Why didn't Liberty simply issue the new song and a new number?

With Smith's first production, "Look At Me Girl", Bobby's records immediately took on a decidedly country/folk flavor, unlike Snuff Garrett's work. In the recent past, music tastes had evolved from early rock and roll to Motown to British Invasion to laid back folk. Now, spaced out psychedelic and countrified folk-rock were invading the airwaves. Changing musically with the times and trends, in terminology of the day, musically speaking, Bobby had gotten a "new bag."

The "Look At Me Girl" record label lists the artist(s) as *Bobby Vee and the Strangers*, although the original Strangers did not perform the backing. Groups were still the norm: The Crycle, The Troggs, The Rascals, Lovin' Spoonful, The Grassroots, and The Byrds, etc... So Liberty again resurrected The Strangers—at least the name—in an apparent attempt to capitalize on group recognition. Bobby's collection of Strangers this time consisted solely of session musicians. In essence, there was little difference between this manifestation of Strangers and The Johnny Mann Singers of old. The record's significance was the familiar Bobby Vee voice, not the unknown voices in the background.

In general, popular music had taken a decidedly harder edge with hard rock bands like the Stones, Yardbirds and Kinks being joined by Cream and Steppenwolf, which were on the rise. If anything, Smith's arrangements were more closely associated with the softer sounds of the Byrds than to these other groups.

Many performers from the early 60's who'd been nudged aside were also adapting their music to fit current tastes. Darin struck gold with Tim Hardin's "If I Were a Carpenter" (#8). Johnny Rivers, who'd made it big with his live *Whiskey à Go Go* albums, had recorded his successful *Johnny Rivers Rocks the Folk.* Dion Dimucci (i.e., Dion and the Belmonts; Dion), after a string of top hits for Columbia, had unsuccessfully recorded a handful of blues songs. Barely scratching the surface of the singles' market with his blues offerings, he turned to folk and put together a new band, Dion and the Wanderers (a primary member of the Wanderers was Carlo Mastrangelo, a member of Dion's original doo-wop group the Belmonts. Also, bass player Pete Falciglia performed with the Belmonts on Sabina Records after Dion and the Belmonts split). It seemed only natural that Bobby Vee, who was still actively recording, would evolve in similar fashion.

"Look At Me Girl" is the first Vee song that broke from the strictly pop pattern he'd been following throughout his career. Light and bouncy, it's one of those tunes that linger in your mind even when you're not thinking of it. A popular South Texas band, The Playboys of Edinburg, first recorded the song. It was more in line with the softer hippie influenced sound of the era than either the suddenly outmoded pop or mind-numbing psychedelic fare. Coming in at #52, it was the highest charting single for Bobby in two years. Although the single showed promise, the album of the same name failed to chart.

Smith hadn't pulled off the big hit they'd hoped for, but it was far and away bigger than anything Bobby had done in a very long time.

Nearing the end of the year, "Here Today", a song Bobby pulled off the Beach Boys' highly acclaimed *Pet Sounds* album was released. The Vee version was produced by Dallas Smith and arranged by Leon Russell. It would finish out Bobby's year, but with no success.

Liberty had been more than fair in its treatment of Bobby's output. Until 1967, almost every year saw at least four new 45's placed in front of his adoring fans—even when his records weren't selling all that well.

But for 1967, more than six months would pass before his next single. Finally, an easy listening ballad written by Martha Sharp[65] called "Come Back When You Grow Up" found its way into record shops. The suggestion to record it came to Smith via an Oklahoma City disc jockey who had heard the song, which was a regional hit by Shadden and The King Lears out of Memphis.

During a lull in a Vikki Carr recording session, Bobby eagerly jumped behind the microphone, borrowing studio time and musicians as Vikki took a break. He and Smith knew they had produced a good product, but only time would tell what the fickle record buying public thought of it.

Bobby promoted the song for months as it slowly and steadily conquered new markets. Breaking big in the west, climbing the charts in the east and south, moving to the top in the Midwest. A chunk here, a chunk there, and each week its popularity grew a little more. Because he had not been a major chart contender for several years, it's doubtful that anyone was prepared for the song's success as it rose all the way to #3! Although the song would ultimately prove to be a giant hit, it took much of the year to achieve its lofty position. Years later he said that it became the biggest record of his career.[66]

The record was Bobby's first Top Ten single since "The Night Has A Thousand Eyes" almost five years before. Billboard magazine ranked it #15 of the Top 100 songs of 1967[67]. He could

---

[65] Martha Sharp also wrote the songs "Born a Woman" and "Single Girl" which earned Gold Record status for Sandy Posey. It was commonly, although mistakenly, believed that Posey was a recording pseudonym for Sharp. Sharp eventually became a Warner Brothers executive for its Nashville operation. http://www.poparchives.com.au/161/judy-stone/born-a-woman
[66] Quote from *Bobby Vee* interview. Ronald Sklar. PopEntertainment.com. 1999.

thank his *comeback* to a song with "come back" in its title. The similarly named album also charted at a very impressive #66.

Riding high on his latest successes, Liberty chose for his next single a faster tempo melody called "Beautiful People". Bobby didn't want to cover yet another singer's record, especially after covering the Playboys of Edinburg song the previous year and more recently Shadden and the King Lears, but Liberty execs put out the record just the same. There's no doubt that "Beautiful People" would have charted much higher, but the song's composer, Kenny O'Dell, had released his own version but a few months before. The two songs went head to head, splitting airplay. O'Dell's version went to #38, one number beyond Bobby's #37. Thus, neither the Vee nor the O'Dell version became the giant hit it might have been.

But Liberty was quick to capitalize on Bobby's recent showing and wanted to get another record out before the end of the year.

On a roll now with airplay, sales and chart positioning, Vee and Smith went to the proverbial well a second time for another Martha Sharp song, hoping to strike lightning again with "Maybe Just Today". Much like his previous releases under Smith's guidance, the song had a measured, almost lethargic feel. Bobby loved the pleasant tune, but admittedly was disappointed in his performance. He would remark about it, "it was like I forgot how to sing—I forgot how to be natural. I've done that a few times in my singing life, where I just wake up and I don't know how to do it anymore."[68] Bobby went on to say, "(I) never should have even put the thing out. It's not a bad record, but..."

If, as he said, he'd "forgotten how to sing", repeated listening to the song fails to reveal any weaknesses in its presentation. Contrary to Bobby's overly critical self-evaluation, it's one of

---

[67] In their singles compilation book, *The Top Ten 1956-Present*, Bob Gilbert and Gary Theroux list "Come Back When You Grow Up" as an even loftier #13 record for 1967.

[68] Bobby went so far as to rerecord "Maybe Just Today", going down half a key and trying it again. Information taken from CD liners notes *Bobby Vee Legendary Masters Series*. Two different versions of the song exist.

those songs that the more I hear it, the more I like it. The record charted at #46, a very reasonable showing.

In my opinion the Dallas Smith produced songs have a more predictable, similar sound, unlike Bobby's earlier releases that were more varied in format. In no way are "Take Good Care of My Baby", "Run to Him", "The Night Has A Thousand Eyes", "Anonymous Phone Call", "Someday", "Yesterday and You", "Stranger In Your Arms", "Never Love a Robin", "Stayin' In", "Walking With My Angel", "Charms", "More Than I Can Say" and most of the others in any way even remotely similar. But I do find similarities in many of the Smith produced material.

From a personal standpoint, I have to separate the Snuff Garrett era from the Dallas Smith. Musically, it's like there are two Bobby Vees—the Garrett produced Brill Building Bobby and the Smith produced folk/country-oriented Bobby. Although his newer music was still considered pop, it had a different ambience. After ten years of often-mellow hit recordings, he had pretty much come full circle back to a more country/down home sound—something like one might expect to hear up in Fargo.

Author's remark: *I grew up listening to the young Bobby Vee sound—the Brill Building pop Bobby. It took a while for me to fully appreciate his later recordings. As I began to research for this book and to carefully listen to his later recordings, I've come to appreciate them far more. Yes, the music has a different feel and sound, more countrified, but that's how his music had evolved. When I hear it juxtaposed to other music of the time, I appreciate it far more than I previously had. It was an evolution of the singer and there's as much brilliance in his late 60's work as in his early 60's. I suggest that anyone who is only familiar with his music from the early years get hold of his later work. You won't be disappointed.*

Although Bobby had been doing the song for some time when on the road, seemingly from out of nowhere came the intriguing medley, "My Girl/Hey Girl". It evoked memories of his hit years and his frequent pairing of Goffin-King tunes. "Hey

Girl" is in fact a Gerry Goffin-Carole King tune that reached #10 for Freddie Scott in 1963, #9 for Donnie Osmond in 1972 and #13 for Billy Joel in 1997! It was the perfect song for the Vee voice and it paired delightfully with the Temptations' 1965 #1 hit, "My Girl".

If it seems a far cry from the Dallas Smith produced recordings, it is. It was produced by pianist/conductor/composer Lincoln Mayorga, who had performed with The Mystic Moods Orchestra[69] and The Piltdown Men.[70] Mayorga had also arranged many songs for his high school friends, the famous pop/folk group the Four Preps.[71] With this release, The Strangers' name had again disappeared from the record label.

"My Girl/Hey Girl" was Bobby's last Top 40 record, topping out at #35 and selling half-a-million units. Interestingly, the B-side was his very good version of an old Dee Clark hit, "Just Keep It Up (See What Happens). Although a wonderful interpretation, it seemed like it was perhaps a year or two too late—but it would have been a perfect fit on an R&B LP.

Here we need pause and take a closer look at what Liberty was doing with regard to Bobby's recent album releases. The *Just Today* and *Do What You Gotta Do* albums are confusing, to say the least.

The general overall sound of America's music was again changing. One faction was the Steppenwolf, Hendrix, Cream heavier side while the other was a softer, somewhat more folk/countrified sound like that of Scott McKenzie, Gary Puckett and the Turtles. Bobby Vee's recordings fit more closely with the latter.

The success of the single "Maybe Just Today" warranted an album release and Liberty would have served the single well by

[69] The Mystic Moods Orchestra released a widely popular series of instrumental albums, blending popular music and environmental sounds, throughout the 1960's and 70's, with the recordings reissued into the 1990's.
[70] Instrumental rock band The Piltdown Men had scored with "Brontosaurus Stomp" and "McDonald's Cave" in 1960.
[71] The Four Preps were Capital Records recording artists, generally folk-oriented whose biggest hits were "Twenty-six Miles", #2 in 1958 and "Big Man", #3 in 1960.

putting out an entire LP of similar songs. However, Bobby's next single, somewhat of a dark horse, was the "My Girl/Hey Girl" medley. It also sold well and Liberty found itself in a dilemma, as the two records were strikingly different. In a head-scratching move, the label proceeded to put both vastly different songs on the *Just Today* album.

With a surprise #35 showing of "My Girl/Hey Girl", Liberty was wise to capitalize on the single's success. It's apparent the company believed they were on to something with Bobby's R&B hit medley and several Motown flavored tunes were recorded. One can only surmise that a complete album of this nature was being considered. But instead of releasing an entire R&B album, the company put out a disorganized mix of similar Motown-like recordings and the rest more in line with the softer "Maybe Just Today" offering. Apparently it worked because the album *Just Today* charted at #187. It was his last album to make the Billboard Top 200.

However, as an earlier song title remarked, Liberty missed its "golden chance" to capitalize on both singles. I contend that many record buyers believed they were getting an album of songs similar to the disc's title and were dismayed to find it half-filled with Motown covers. Liberty execs might have been wiser to release an entire R&B album titled *My Girl/Hey Girl* and follow it up shortly with his next LP, *Do What You Gotta Do*, complete with the "Maybe Just Today" hit single and the softer, original songs that were sprinkled on the *Just Today* disc. Half the tracks on the album were also in the Motown vein, thus ensuring it to be as disjointed as the previous disc.

I don't find the R&B tracks all that desirable (and perhaps that's because there have been so many attempts by others to cover the songs). Admittedly there are some good tracks besides "My Girl/Hey Girl" and "Just Keep it Up", but even a similar medley attempt at combining the Four Tops splendid classics "I Can't Help Myself/The Same Old Song", does not capture the freshness of "My Girl/Hey Girl". If, and this is only conjecture, a R&B LP was planned, I believe it would have been merely mediocre and not up to the very high standards we were accustomed to. Regardless, of what might have been done with those tracks, the best songs on the *Just Today* and *Do What You Gotta Do* albums were the new tracks. Eliminating the R&B songs and combining the new tracks into a single album could have produced a very special disc, indeed.

Perfect for the LP however were the songs "Tiffany Rings" and "Sunrise Highway", the latter being an interesting and delightful Peter Andreoli and Vini Poncia composition[72] that was on the *Just Today* album. These songs and similar others should have supplanted the R&B offerings. Very reminiscent of "Charms", "Tiffany Rings", is one of those melodies that grow on you the more you hear it. "Nobody's Home to Go Home To" is another beautiful ballad done up in Bobby's special way. It's fresh and sweet with just the right touch of moderate rhythm to keep the subject from becoming glum. If Liberty had any intention of steering Bobby to an older audience, it certainly fit the bill.

Had Liberty had the foresight to release two distinctly separate albums with songs more appropriate to the hit song they supported, I'm certain Bobby's fans would have appreciated the gesture and the company would have achieved significantly higher sales. This is entirely speculation, but it's a more logical concept than releasing two fragmented albums that were almost identical in their makeup. Enough Motown covers existed for a strictly R&B album and the remaining songs were sufficient to fill a non R&B disc. Thus, two separate, but cohesive albums. Although Bobby's musical offerings are of his always-high quality, Liberty expended very little thought, imagination and effort in preparing these two LPs.

Along with his excellent rendition of the title song for his *Do What You Gotta Do* album, "Can You Love a Poor Boy" evokes

---

[72] Peter Andreoli and Vini Poncia were prolific songwriters, record producers and recording artists who performed under a variety of names: Anders and Poncia, Pete and Vini, the Innocence, the Videls and the Tradewinds—garnering a moderate hit with "New York's a Lonely Town" under the latter name in 1965. Look for a future book exploring the work of these two individuals.

memories of his beautiful love ballads of earlier years. This is one of those songs that certainly could have been a hit in years past. Of further note on the LP is the reworking of Bobby's 1965 vastly underrated and overlooked gem, "Run Like the Devil". The original recording had failed to chart, reaching only a dismal #124 on Billboard's Bubbling Under chart. It's an excellent song and very puzzling why it did not soar high up the charts. The new version is given a very Motownish bass backbeat replete with horns, which makes one wonder if it, too, was intended for inclusion on an R&B album. Regardless of the intention, the original version is the stronger of the two.

While Bobby's performance on the material was as excellent as always, I believe Liberty's support for the two discs was lackluster. Not only is the content of both albums vastly similar, it appears that Liberty used photos from the same photo-shoot for the covers. Upon close inspection of the two covers, Bobby is wearing the same white turtleneck in front of the same mottled blue background. Liberty appeared to be just going through the motions with these two LPs.

But after the surprise showing for "My Girl/Hey Girl", Bobby Vee's singles again began a slow descent into the deeper reaches of the Top 100. The excellent, but widely covered single "Do What You Gotta Do" slid to #83, and "(I'm Into Lookin' For) Someone To Love Me" #98.

In another quirky twist of band name irony, the UK group The Shadows, of which Bobby's band had relinquished their name and become The Strangers, took into their group John Farrar,[73] an Australian musician who had most recently worked with an Aussie band named the Strangers!

Bobby's sole single of 1969, "Let's Call It A Day Girl", #92, was an admirable cover of the Razor's Edge[74] '66 release on the

---

[73] Australian born musician/producer/songwriter/arranger John Farrar, became most famous for his association with Cliff Richard and the Shadows AND for producing Olivia Newton John's number-one LPs, *If You Love Me, Let Me Know; Have You Never Been Mello;* and *Olivia's Greatest Hits, Vol. 2,* plus producing Grammy Award winning Record of the Year 1975, for "I Honestly Love You".

[74] The Razor's Edge was a mid-60's 4-Seasons/Happenings sound-alike group. It's a mystery why the

independent Pow! Records label. It was a perfect choice for Bobby's voice. Energetic, catchy and very much in "The Night Has A Thousand Eyes" vein. It's unfortunate that it did not become a hit. Five-years earlier, and given adequate airplay, I'm sure it would have.

But major changes were brewing at Liberty's corporate level. In 1969, Liberty Records would merge with co-owned United Artists and its subsidiary Imperial Records. As the folk trifecta Zimmerman/Gunn/Dylan had written earlier, *the times they are a-changing.*[75]

Bobby's "In and Out Of Love" followed in 1970, but it only charted on the Bubbling Under Hot 100 at #111. It's a fine mid tempo, Snuff Garrett produced ballad. With the unfailingly excellent Ernie Freeman now gone, Al Capps arranged the song.[76] The old guard that brought Liberty years of constant hits had pretty much dissipated—taking their talents with them.

By now there was little consistency to Bobby's production team, unlike the old days when Snuff Garrett was his sole producer. Releases during this time were often split between Smith and Garrett (perhaps salvaging older tracks that had not been released during Snuff's tenure), although Dallas Smith had become the primary director for Bobby's records.

Puzzling as it might be, Liberty released the LP, *Gates, Grills and Railings*. Although "Let's Call It A Day Girl" had charted low on the Top 100, that being the only song with even marginal name recognition, it was not included on the album. The disk did have an interesting and potentially strong track lineup with a couple Carole Bayer songs, covers of Three Dog Night's "One", John Sebastian's "Younger Generation", and the B.J. Thomas classic "I

---

group did not catch on as their limited offerings had immense potential: "Let's Call If A Day Girl"; "Night and Day" (a reworking of the old Cole Porter chestnut); "Don't Let Me Catch You In His Arms"; and an exceptional "Pollyanna".

[75] Lyrics from *The Times They Are A-Changin'*, by Bob Dylan, Special Rider Music.

[76] Liberty may once again have been trying to steer Bobby's career into a more adult format. Capps seemed more likely associated with MOR artists like Andy Williams, Vikki Carr, Helen Reddy, Liza Minnelli, The Osmonds, The Lennon Sisters and Jennifer Warnes.

Just Can't Help Believin'." The LP embraced a very strong lineup with spot on Vee interpretations.

As mentioned earlier, the talents of Bobby Vee and the UK's Cliff Richard seemed to cross paths quite often, with Bobby and Cliff making similar recordings along the way. Here, Bobby does his own interpretation of Cliff's album track "London's Not Too Far", which was written by Hank B. Marvin. Marvin, known primarily for his guitar prowess, influencing such greats as Eric Clapton, George Harrison, Mark Knopler, Peter Frampton and many others, also recorded a vocal version of his song. Marvin was in fact the lead guitarist of the UK's Shadows, the group that caused Bobby's band to rename itself The Strangers.

As solid as Bobby's album was, unfortunately, it did not chart.

The single "Sweet Sweetheart" finished out 1970. A Goffin-King composition in a light country mode, it certainly equaled much of the country rock that saturated the airwaves. With shuffling guitar intro *à la* Roy Orbison's "Dream Baby (How Long Must I Dream)", the Dallas Smith produced single charted at #88—the final time Bobby Vee's name would grace the Top 100 charts.

***

With that, Bobby Vee and Liberty Records closed the door on their extremely successful 14-yr partnership. Thirty-eight Bobby Vee singles scored in the Top 100. One achieved the very top spot. Several others ranked in the Top Five. Also, several of his albums placed high in the charts. During those fourteen years he'd gone from a budding local celebrity to an international star. But now, Bobby and the only major label he'd ever known were parting ways.

In 1971, United Artists released the Bobby Vee single "Signs" and his album *Nothin' Like A Sunny Day* in 1972. Neither record charted. After all his years as Bobby Vee, the album listed Robert Thomas Velline as the artist and showed a bearded, mature

Velline on the album cover. That should have removed any doubt that his Liberty association was a thing of the past.

Perhaps the most notable song on the ...*Sunny Day* disc was a slowed down adaptation of "Take Good Care of My Baby". After hearing the original for so many years it takes getting used to hearing it at a different tempo. Once you overcome that you see it simply as another wonderful Bobby Vee song—two very different songs (except the lyrics are the same).

Regarding the makeup of the album, six of the songs are Robert Thomas Velline compositions—another sign the young Bobby was slipping further into the past. Fittingly, this was his last original LP issued by a major record company.[77]

United Artists released the slowed down version of "Take Good Care of My Baby" as a single in 1972, but it died with little fanfare. And with that, the last train left the station for Bobby Vee and United Artists.

A rerecording of Buddy Holly's "Well, All Right" was made for Bobby's *I Remember Buddy Holly* CD. It was his second recording of the song, having recorded it ten years earlier for his *Meets the Crickets* LP. Released in 1978, after 19-years and a brief departure, it was his final track for Liberty records.

United Artists went on to release some compilation albums of mainly earlier hits and in future years, as compact discs began to hit the stores, there would be many reissues and various compilation and collectors albums. In fact, most of the Bobby Vee catalog has been reissued, often many times over. A 2011 United Kingdom CD entitled *Rarities* offers collectors many previously unreleased tracks and many of the reissue CDs include unreleased material or different takes than the original. Ironically, the full catalog of Bobby Vee material is more readily available today than it was when Bobby Vee's name was a constant on record industry charts.

---

[77] After several years, Bobby Vee occasionally released new projects through his independent Rockhouse label, which the Vee family founded in 1989.

The Music of Bobby Vee

9

STELLAR CAREER WINDS DOWN

Bobby was content to let his U.A. contract run out with no further releases. A few years later the tiny independent label Shady Brook recorded a handful of tracks (released in 1975 and '76) and for the Cognito label two more (1979). The records, if you can find them, are indeed rare.

The U.A. Silver Spotlight Series and Collectables would both rerelease two-sided hit 45 rpms. Several of his albums would be reissued in CD format, many with additional, unreleased tracks or alternate takes. There's plenty of Bobby's material available if one only looks for it.

Bobby Vee placed 38 singles in the Billboard Top 100 charts (22 of them between 1960-63—an almost unheard of achievement), 14 Top Forty hits, seven Gold singles, and two Gold albums, all on Liberty, putting him perhaps in a class with Elvis Presley, Pat Boone and Jackie Wilson for longevity with one label. Most of his contemporaries changed labels multiples times. Legends Roy Orbison, Dion and Del Shannon did so, for whatever that matters.

Bobby scored a number one, number two and two number three singles and placed nine records in the Top Twenty. A dozen Vee albums graced Billboard's top LP chart. He shared the stage with Bob Dylan and stood behind a mic with Leon Russell before either of these two rock giants gained individual fame. His collaboration with The Crickets almost reached the top of the UK's album charts.

The record trade magazine *Billboard* called Bobby Vee "One of the top ten most consistent chart makers ever." His was a phenomenal career.

As with many popular singers of the era, Bobby had singing roles in teen-oriented films such as *Swingin' Along* (1962), *Play It Cool* (1962) and *Just For Fun* (1963)—The Crickets, Jet Harris and Tony Meehan of England's original Shadows also appear in the latter film.

Generally only the very top names were offered starring roles: Presley, Pat Boone, Bobby Darin, Frankie Avalon and Cliff Richard in the UK would all star in an array of films. Fabian, Connie Francis and Rick Nelson also found their way into significant screen roles, but mostly a singer's role was a cameo performing one or two songs.

Oddly, long after his days of surefire hits were past, Bobby starred as a college bound country boy with songwriter/singer extraordinaire Jackie DeShannon in the 1967 film, *C'mon Let's Live a Little*. Eddie Hodges and Kim Carnes also had roles.

TV music shows like *Shindig, Hollywood a Go Go*, *Where the Action Is*, *The Clay Cole Show*, *The Midnight Special*, *Happening '68* and other shows frequently hosted Bobby and he was a staple on Dick Clark's *American Bandstand. He showed up on 1968's Macy's Thanksgiving Day Parade, 1978's Sha Na Na* and a *1979 Hollywood Squares* segment, with contemporaries Connie Francis, Fabian, Frankie Avalon, Patti Page, Freddy Cannon, Little Anthony, Martha Reeves and the legendary Dick Clark taking the center square.

In 1985, Bobby toured England with contemporaries Del Shannon and Rick Nelson. Others on the bill were Frankie Ford, Bo Diddley and a new group performing as the Marvelettes. The tour entourage performed about a dozen sold-out shows throughout the Kingdom and were wildly received. Forever popular overseas, Bobby continued to tour Europe until he retired.

When eldest son Jeff turned 16, Bobby and Karen decided to return to the Midwest, so they up and moved from California back to the Detroit Lakes area, east of Fargo. The family had always considered the area their second home and made summer pilgrimages to their cabin.

"It probably would have been better for Dad's career if they (the family) had stayed in California," son Jeff said in a 2012 interview. "But they wanted us to have those Midwest values."[78]

With the move, gone were the days of balmy California sunshine and frequent visits to Dick Clark's home for barbecues.

Tommy Vee would recall growing up in California as normal being around people in the music industry—singers, writers, and musicians. He and his brothers attended school with kids from other famous families: Bob Newhart, Carroll O'Connor, Jerry Lewis, etc. The boys only came to realize their dad's star status after moving to Minnesota and Bobby being the only celebrity in town.

Bobby and Karen's multi-talented sons, Tom and Jeff, would form the Vees, performing as Bobby's backup band and on their own—often teaming up with Rick Nelson's twin sons doing Ricky Nelson tribute concerts. Son Robby, named after his father and known as "The Prince of Twang", is a widely acclaimed rock and roll guitarist. He's a member of both the American and Canadian Rockabilly Halls of Fame. The Vee family owns and operates Rockhouse Productions, LLC and recording studio in St. Joseph, northwest of Minneapolis.

The stately old beige and brown brick building on the corner that houses the studio was once the local First State Bank. For many years' sons Jeff and Tommy managed their father's career until Bobby retired. The boys now operate the studio, manage, book and record various acts in the region.

In 2005, Bobby and sons went in their recording studio and put together an astoundingly good CD, *The Last of the Great Rhythm Guitar Players*. Bobby wrote all of the songs except for the last two, which are his slowed down versions of his earlier big hits.

Excluding the slowed versions of his hit songs that are found on previous CDs, perhaps the true gem of this set is the bluesy

[78] Jeff Vee quote extracted from Business Central (For Business Leaders of Central Minnesota – St. Cloud Chamber of Commerce) January/February 2012, by Gail Ivers.

"Kansas City…Do Wa Do". It's Bobby as we've never heard him before—and how we should have heard him more often. That being said, this CD is so tight that one can simply pick any of the songs at random and come up with a classic: "Don't Let Your Dreams Go", "What She Sees in Him", "I Wouldn't Change A Thing", and any of the rest. It's that good of an album.

If a person wants to know how Bobby sums up his life and his career, simply listen to his self-penned "I Wouldn't Change A Thing". It pretty much tells it all in less than four minutes. The song compares favorably with anything he ever recorded—and exceeds most of it.

With a trace of melancholy in the liner notes, Bobby dedicates the CD to his departed siblings, Bill and Syd Junior, nephew Ronnie and his "friend Charles Westover"—we know him as Del Shannon.

Fittingly, the CD's monochrome cover photo shows a solemn Bobby dressed in black with the grass covered rolling hills of Theodore Roosevelt National Park as the backdrop.

Bobby was honored as the 30th recipient of North Dakota's prestigious Teddy Roosevelt Rough Rider Award in June 1999. The back cover, however, shows him flashing his ever-youthful, always optimistic smile.

***

For two-and-a-half years Bobby performed in the Ozark Mountains' family entertainment destination, Branson, Missouri, sharing stage with rock legends at scenic Branson's Dick Clark American Bandstand Theater.

Touring in the USA and Europe, where is still immensely popular, Bobby performed more than 100 concerts a year. That grueling schedule only slowed him when the early stages of Alzheimer's disease began.

***

Bobby and his sons met up in Tucson in 2014 to lay down tracks for what became *The Adobe Sessions* album. It contained a generous mix of oldies, new material and old favorites like "In My

Baby's Eyes", Rick Nelson's "Never Be Anyone Else But You", and Don Williams' "I'm Just a Country Boy". In all likelihood "Father To a Son" is a tribute to his beloved family—his musical legacy. As the song goes "it's a simple truth…"

In true fashion, Bobby wouldn't let his final album pass without recognizing Buddy Holly with his own version of "Love Must Have Passed Me By".

Bobby Vee, a genuine gentleman and incredible entertainer, a legend in pop/rock music, recorded his final album and then slipped quietly into retirement.

The Music of Bobby Vee

PART TWO

10

ALBUMS

This chapter looks at Bobby's album releases, but does not take into account the various compilations that would be released over time. The label number (both mono and stereo numbers when appropriate), year of release and highest chart position are listed.[79] Although this chapter is primarily dedicated to Bobby Vee's U.S. album releases, because of his extensive catalog and many superb recordings, a select few overseas releases are mentioned if they offer material that is not readily available in the USA.

***

1960—Bobby Vee Sings Your Favorites (Liberty LRP-3165/LST-7165): Devil Or Angel • Mr. Blue • Just A Dream • Since I Met You Baby • It's All In The Game • You Send Me • Young Love • My Prayer • Sincerely • Gone • I'm Sorry • Everyday

Commentary: Bobby's first album contains a dozen ballads, consisting of old standards and "newer" love songs. It capitalized on the success of the #6 charting "Devil or Angel". Initially, Vee recorded six rock numbers at Norman Petty's Studio in Clovis, NM. Six ballads recorded at United Studios in Los Angeles were to share vinyl on the album, but producer Snuff Garrett was so

---

[79] Record trade magazines such as Billboard and Cashbox, compiled chart positions based on sales. Singles were compiled on a Hot 100 list and albums on the Top 200. The weekly record industry periodicals presented other, less extensive charts for categories such as Country and Western and Rhythm and Blues, but they are not relevant to this work.

taken by the full orchestral offerings at United, that he scrapped the rock numbers. The album provides a good look at popular ballads during that period and what fans could expect from Bobby on future recordings.

1961—Bobby Vee (Liberty LRP-3181/LST-7181) (3-61, #18)(1961): Rubber Ball • Talk To Me Talk To Me • One Last Kiss • Angels In The Sky • Stayin' In • Long Lonely Nights • Devil Or Angel • Poetry In Motion • More Than I Can Say • Mister Sandman • Foolish Tears • Love Love Love

Commentary: It's more up-tempo than his first album, with a generous mix of original hits and contemporary covers. The album reached #18. "Rubber Ball" was co-written by Aaron Schroeder and rising recording star Gene Pitney, (who used his mother's name to avoid a conflict of interest).

1961—Bobby Vee With Strings and Things (Liberty LRP-3186/LST-7186): Baby Face • Pledging My Love • Love's Made A Fool of You • Light Infatuation • Susie-Q • Tears On My Pillow • How Many Tears • That's All • Diana • Laurie • Each Night • Bashful Bob

Commentary: Similar to his second album, with a mix of covers and original material. Bobby covers another Holly song, "Love's Made A Fool of You". We would see this throughout his career—Bobby covering Holly material.

Hits of the Rockin' Fifties (1961): (Liberty LRP-3205/LST-7205 [1961] (10-61, #85): *Rhythm Side:* Do You Wanna Dance • Lollipop • School Days • Little Star • Come Go With Me • Summertime Blues *Ballad Side:* Happy Happy Birthday Baby • Lavender Blue • Donna • Earth Angel • Wisdom Of A Fool • Sixteen Candles

Commentary: The album consists of half rockers and half ballads. No original Vee material on the disc, but with a very strong cast of songs it rose to #85. The Five Keys' "Wisdom of A Fool" is perhaps the jewel of the set.

1961—Teensville (Liberty L-5503): Bashful Bob - Bobby Vee • Everyday - Bobby Vee • One Last Kiss - Bobby Vee • Raindrops, Teardrops - The Fleetwoods • The Little White Cloud That Cried - The Fleetwoods • Truly Do - The Fleetwoods • I'm Still Dreamin' - Johnny Burnette • It's Only Make Believe - Johnny Burnette • My Special Angel - Johnny Burnette • No Trespassing - The Ventures • Ram-Bunk-Shush - The Ventures • Rawhide - The Ventures

Commentary: This is a various artist's budget compilation of Liberty and its Dolton subsidiary artists. Three songs are by Bobby Vee. All tracks on the disc were previously released. Albums of this nature were meant purely to attract additional sales by showcasing the label's talent. None of the tracks were major hits by any of these artists.

1961—Take Good Care of My Baby Liberty LRP-3211/LST-7211) (2-62, #91): Take Good Care Of My Baby • Will You Love Me Tomorrow • Remember Me Huh • He Will Break Your Heart • Who Am I • Run To Him • Walkin' With My Angel • Raining In My Heart • Go On • Little Flame • So You're In Love • Hark Is That A Cannon I Hear

Commentary: The strongest Bobby Vee album to date, although still using the proven formula of mixing the latest original hit(s) with new material and covers. With the #1 title track and its #2 follow-up as the main enticements, it came in at #91. Bobby's rendition of Holly's beautiful "Raining in My Heart" highlighted the array of excellent tracks.

1962—Bobby Vee Meets the Crickets (Liberty LRP-3228/LST-7228) (7- 62, #42): Peggy Sue • Bo Diddley • Someday • Well All Right • I Gotta Know • Lookin' For Love • Sweet Little Sixteen • When You're In Love • Lucille • The Girl Of My Best Friend • Little Queenie • The Girl Can't Help It

Commentary: Easily Bobby Vee's hardest rocking LP with a superb set of great Holly, Chuck Berry, and Little Richard tracks, as he teams up with Holly's own Crickets. It's difficult to find a weak track on the entire album. "Someday", "When You're in Love", "Little Queenie" and "Sweet Little Sixteen" are perhaps the finest tracks. Jerry Allison's unmistakable frenetic drumming resonates throughout the entire disc. Combining Vee and The Crickets, who were now also under contract with Liberty, was sheer brilliance resulting in the second highest LP chart position of his career to that point. In England, the album soared all the way to #2. (The compact disc reissue release of this album includes several previously unreleased tracks with the Crickets). Recording with the Crickets, the Ventures, a Buddy Holly tribute LP, and his *30 Hits of the 60's* albums, a good argument can be made that Bobby Vee was one of the originators of concept albums.

1962—A Bobby Vee Recording Session (Liberty LRP-3232/LST-7232) (7-62, #121): What's Your Name • My Golden Chance • You Better Move On • Please Don't Ask About Barbara • Forget Me Not • Sharing You • In My Baby's Eyes • Tenderly Yours • I Can't Say Goodbye • Teardrops Fall Like Rain • Guess Who • A Forever Kind Of Love

Commentary: Another strong showing with "Please Don't Ask About Barbara", "Sharing You", "In My Baby's Eyes", and a marvelous Crickets' tune, "Teardrops Fall Like Rain". Renowned British record producer/arranger/composer/orchestral conductor Norrie Paramor arranged "A Forever Kind of Love". Paramor also arranged Cliff Richard's version of the same song slightly earlier than Bobby Vee's, but Richard's version was not released at the time. Due to Bobby's #13 UK hit with the song, Cliff Richard's version would not be released for another two years.

1962—Bobby Vee's Golden Greats (Liberty LRP-3245/LST-7245) (11-62, #24): Take Good Care Of My Baby • Devil Or Angel • Punish Her • Suzie Baby • Walkin' With My Angel • Stayin' In • Run To Him • Rubber Ball • Please Don't Ask About Barbara • How Many Tears • Everyday • Sharing You • One Last Kiss • More Than I Can Say • Someday

Commentary: All of his hits up to that point. It includes "Punish Her", which had not appeared on any other LP up to that point. It's a "can't go wrong" LP.

1962—Merry Christmas From Bobby Vee (1962): (Liberty LRP-3267/LST-7267) (12-62, #136): White Christmas • Silent Night • Silver Bells • My Christmas Love • (There's No Place Like) Home For The Holidays • Winter Wonderland • Blue Christmas • I'll Be Home For Christmas • Jingle Bell Rock • A Not So Merry Christmas

Commentary: Surpasses expectations. "Silver Bells", "I'll Be Home For Christmas", "A Not So Merry Christmas" and "(There's No Place Like) Home For the Holidays" are among many superb holiday songs, both standards and new offerings. The 1992 compact disc release of this album includes "A Christmas Wish", "Christmas Vacation" and the excellent "Electric Trains and You"—all splendid additions to an already excellent album.

1963—The Night Has A Thousand Eyes (1963): (Liberty LRP-3285/LST-7285) (4-63, #102): Go Away Little Girl • It Might As Well Rain Until September • It Couldn't Happen To A Nicer Guy • Theme For A Dream • Silent Partner • The Night Has A Thousand Eyes • You Won't Forget Me • Anonymous Phone Call • If She

Were My Girl • Lover's Goodbye • Dry Your Eyes • What About Me

Commentary: Excellent Vee versions of Carole King's "It Might As Well Rain Until September", Cliff Richard's "Theme For a Dream" and Jackie DeShannon's "You Won't Forget Me". One wonders why his then current single, "Charms", was not included, as it was released shortly before the album. It undoubtedly would have helped drive sales. Some excellent, fairly unnoticed tracks include "It Couldn't Happen to A Nicer Guy" and "Anonymous Phone Call". The album achieved a decent charting, coming within only two points from breaking into the Hot 100.

1963—Bobby Vee Meets the Ventures (1963): (Liberty LRP-3289/LST-7289) (6-63, #91): Wild Night • What Else Is New • Walk Right Back • This Is Where Friendship Ends • Pretty Girls Everywhere • Linda Lu • If I'm Right Or Wrong • I'm Gonna Sit Right Down And Write Myself A Letter • Honeycomb • Goodnight Irene • Caravan • Candy Man

Commentary: This album charted much higher than his two previous releases. It seems Liberty tried to recapture the success of Bobby's *Meets the Crickets* LP, but it didn't have the same chemistry. The Ventures were perhaps the best instrumental group of the time and "Walk, Don't Run" is one of the all-time great guitar instrumentals (peaking at #2 in 1960 and an updated, surf influenced remake called "Walk, Don't Run '64", reached #8 four years later). Their melding with Bobby didn't come off nearly as smoothly as that with The Crickets. Liberty's Ventures venture seemed contrived. Two songs on the album, "Wild Night" and "Caravan", are strictly instrumentals.

1963—I Remember Buddy Holly (Liberty LRP-3336/LST-7336): That'll Be The Day • It Doesn't Matter Anymore • Peggy Sue • True Love Ways • It's So Easy • Heartbeat • Oh Boy •

Raining In My Heart • Think It Over • Maybe Baby • Early In The Morning • Buddy's Song

Commentary: A natural offering giving tribute to his idol, Bobby pulls it off nicely. Beginning with his very first LP, Bobby routinely covered Holly songs with Buddy's tunes popping up quite frequently. This is practically a "Greatest Hits" album, but with the fan covering the idol. It's an exceptional mix of classic ballads and rockers with Buddy's influence reflected in Bobby's treatment of the songs.

1964—The New Sound From England! (1964): (Liberty LRP-3352/LST-7352) (6-64, #146): I'll Make You Mine • Don't You Believe Them • She Loves You • I'll String Along With You • Ginger • Any Other Girl • She's Sorry • Brown-Eyed Handsome Man • Suspicion • From Me To You • You Can't Lie To A Liar • Take A Walk Johnny

Commentary: With the British Invasion having hit our shores, radio stations were intent on saturating the airwaves with overseas groups to the detriment of U.S. artists. Del Shannon recognized the British influence early and recorded a Beatles' tune, "From Me to You". Attempting to capitalize on the new sound, Liberty released this album. It was reasonably successful and made it to #146 on the charts. "I'll Make You Mine" was the showcase of the album and certainly captured the British sound. It was Bobby's biggest hit in the past year, although only achieving #52. Arguably, it is a much better song than many British Invasion records that were being played on popular radio. Bobby covers two Beatles' songs. Noted on the back cover "Vocal background by The Eligibles."

1964—30 Big Hits of the 60's (Liberty LRP-3385/LST-7385): Dawn • Moon River • Danke Schoen • Memphis • I Remember You • Sukiyaki • Save The Last Dance For Me • Do You Want To Know A Secret? • Needles and Pins • P.S. I Love You •

Everybody's Somebody's Fool • My Dad • Venus In Blue Jeans • Happy Birthday Sweet 16 • Hey Girl • Please Help Me I'm Falling • Blame It On The Bossa Nova • Crying In The Rain • Ruby Baby • Sealed With A Kiss • Breaking Up Is Hard to Do • Nadine • Goodbye Cruel World • Blue On Blue • Can't Get Used to Losing You • Love Me Do • A Fool Never Learns • Spanish Harlem • Twist And Shout

Commentary: A veritable What's What of early 60's hit songs. Some of the tracks are abbreviated versions in order to get that many tracks onto the vinyl record, but the album certainly showcases Bobby's ability to sing almost any kind of song with great success. Among the 30 tracks are several Beatles, a Searchers and a Frank Ifield song. Coming shortly after Bobby's *New Sound From England* LP, perhaps those songs had been considered for that disk but didn't make the cut. This is only speculation.

1965—Live On Tour (1965): (Liberty LRP-3393/LST-7393): Hey Little Girl • Sea Cruise • Things • Shop Around • Let The Four Winds Blow • Weekend • Every Day I Have To Cry • You Must Have Been A Beautiful Baby • It'll Be Me • Run To Him • Take Good Care Of My Baby • The Night Has A Thousand Eyes

Commentary: The British Invasion being in full swing and Bobby not having a significant hit for some time, Liberty released what they dubbed a "live" album of a few of his major hits and the rest covers of other artist's hits. Practically all of the non Bobby Vee songs seem to be a few years outdated, with nothing to link him to the then current music sound. It's not that he doesn't serve the covers up nicely, because he does, but I believe this offering would have worked better by pushing more of his own originals. Regarding "live," the applause is artificially added. *Faux* "live" albums seldom work well regardless of who the artist is.

1966—C'mon, Let's Live a Little (Original Sound Track Recording) (Liberty LRP-3430/LST-7430) Don Ralke: C'mon Let's Live A Little - Opening Main Title • Instant Girl - Bobby Vee • Baker Man - Jackie DeShannon • C'mon Let's Live A Little - Suzie Kaye • What Fool This Mortal Be - Bobby Vee • Tonight's The Night - The Pair • For Granted - Jackie DeShannon • Back-Talk - Bobby Vee & Jackie DeShannon • Over And Over - Bobby Vee • Let's Go Go - Eddie Hodges • Way Back Home - Ethel Smith & Don Crawford • C'mon Let's Live A Little - End Title

Commentary: The most memorable thing about this soundtrack LP is the pairing of Bobby and songwriter/singer extraordinaire Jackie DeShannon. But, like the previous LP, this seems to have come a few years too late for these two exceptional singers. The material is very pedestrian—average at best—but par for most teen movies of that generation.

1966—30 Hits Of The 60's, Vol. 2 (Liberty LRP-3448/LST-7448): A Hundred Pounds Of Clay-Elusive Butterfly/A Taste Of Honey-Wives And Lovers/These Boots Are Made For Walking-Sha La la/Tower Of Strength-The Man Who Shot Liberty Valence/Baby I'm Yours-Make It Easy On Yourself/When You Walk In The Room-The "In" Crowd/Pony Time-You Can Have Her • Lies-Count Me In/Love Is All We Need-Call Me Irresponsible/Bad To Me-I'm A Fool/Save Your Heart For Me-In The Misty Moonlight/The Story Of My Life-Travelin' Man/Mr. Blue-Come Stay With Me/Sandy-For Your Love/Houston-You're Sixteen

Commentary: Like 1964's Vol. 1, these are snippets of past hits of the era. Each song is a medley combining two songs into one. As always, Bobby is in great voice, but this has a feel of Liberty simply trying to capitalize on Bobby's name and fame. An LP of a dozen original offerings might have served him better.

1966—Bobby Vee's Golden Greats, Volume 2 (Liberty LRP-3464/LST-7464): Charms • Cross My Heart • The Night Has A Thousand Eyes • I'll Make You Mine • Never Love A Robin • Armen's Theme [Yesterday And You] • Ev'ry Little Bit Hurts • Hickory Dick And Doc • Keep On Trying • A Girl I Used To Know • Pretend You Don't See Her • Be True To Yourself

Commentary: At last, a second volume of greatest hits! Where was this album two years before? Had it been released in 1964, there was a very strong likelihood it would have charted—and perhaps quite high. However, where are "Stranger In Your Arms", "In My Baby's Eyes", "A Forever Kind of Love", "Someday", and "Anonymous Phone Call?" These additions truly would have made it an LP of "Golden Greats!" It seems that Liberty was only going through the motions on Bobby's last several releases and was no longer fully committed to properly promoting his music.

1966—Look At Me Girl :(Liberty LRP-3480/LST-7480) [1966]: Look At Me Girl • Sunny • Growing Pains • Like You've Never Known Before • Summer In The City • Turn-Down Day • Fly Away • Sweet Pea • That's All In The Past • He's Not Your Friend • Back In Town • Lil' Red Riding Hood

Commentary: This is the album that should have come out in lieu of *30 Hits of the 60's, Vol. 2*. The new/original material is fresh and current and the covers, such as "Sunny" and "Turn Down Day" are in touch with the mid 60's, which this album represents. Actually, the title track is a cover of a song by the 60's South Texas group, The Playboy's of Edinburg. The title song charted at #52, equaling his best showing in two years.

1967—Come Back When You Grow Up (Liberty LRP-3534/LST-7534) [1967] (10-67, #66): Come Back When You Grow Up • A Rose Grew In The Ashes • You're A Big Girl Now • You Can Count On Me • Get The Message • Hold On To Him •

World Down On Your Knees • Objects Of Gold • Before You Go • Mission Accomplished • I May Be Back • Double Good Feeling

Commentary: The single, "Come Back When You Grow Up", brought Bobby back to the top of the singles charts, topping out at #3! Beginning with 1963's "Be True To Yourself", which charted at #34, the highest chart placement for Bobby were three singles that none of which rose higher than #52. It was a surprising comeback for him. Although music in general had changed, this album is reminiscent of the LPs he put out during earlier years, with this material all being fresh and new. Bobby did not rely on the hits of others to boost this album. This one is all his. And coming in at #66 on the album chart, proves that he had again become a force in the music industry.

1968—Just Today (Liberty LRP-3554/LST-7554) (4-68, #187): Maybe Just Today • Get Ready • Medley: My Girl/Hey Girl • Sunrise Highway • Just Keep It Up • The Girl I Left Behind Me • The Way You Do The Things You Do • Nobody's Home To Go Home To • Sealed With A Kiss • Tiffany Rings • Beautiful People

Commentary: This album spawned three moderate hits—or more accurately, three moderate hits are showcased on this LP: "Beautiful People", "Maybe Just Today", and an interesting coupling of "My Girl/Hey Girl". "Tiffany Rings" and "Sunrise Highway" are two of the LP's gems.

1968—Do What You Gotta Do (Liberty LST-7592): Do What You Gotta Do • If My World Falls Through • Thank You • Beauty Is Only Skin Deep • Stubborn Kind Of Fellow • Can You Love A Poor Boy • Medley: I Can't Help Myself (Sugar Pie Honey Bunch)-It's The Same Old Song • I Like It Like That • Run Like The Devil • Let Nobody Love You (While I'm Gone) • That's What Love Is Made Of

Commentary: Bobby does an excellent interpretation of what had already become a standard, with numerous artists covering the Jim Webb[80] classic, "Do What You Gotta Do". Bobby Vee's version is one of the best. It's difficult to understand why "My Girl/Hey Girl" was placed on the previous album and not on this one, as this LP has several Motown covers—which leads one to wonder if a R&B album was considered, but scrapped. It might have been wiser to release an all R&B album instead of putting a handful of these songs on each of the last several albums—and load up the other albums with original material. The records would be much more cohesive. The excellent, although ill-fated "Run Like the Devil" is included on this disk. "Can You Love a Poor Boy" is reminiscent of Bobby's mid-sixties work. It's a very good song on a good album. The LP cover is similar to Donovan's *Sunshine Superman* LP with colorful butterflies and psychedelic-like artwork. It appears Bobby's photo came from the same photo-shoot as the cover for its predecessor. Both covers display a mottled bluish background and Bobby wears the same white turtleneck. It's impossible to understand what Liberty was thinking on his last several albums.

1969—Gates, Grills And Railings (Liberty LST-7612): She Doesn't Live Here Anymore • The Passing Of A Friend • One • (I'm Into Lookin' For) Someone To Love Me • London's Not Too Far • Younger Generation • I Just Can't Help Believin' • Jenny Come To Me • Lavender Kite • The Beauty And The Sweet Talk • Santa Cruz • Annie Joined The Band

Commentary: Perhaps one of his more contemporary offerings during the late 60's. It teases with the Hank Marvin composed

---

[80] Jim Webb was a prolific song writer who penned countless major hits: "By the Time I Get to Phoenix", "Wichita Lineman", "MacArthur Park", "Up, Up and Away", "Galveston", "Didn't We", "Early Morning Song", "Highwayman", "The Moon Is A Harsh Mistress", "Honey Come Back" and many more. Among others, "Do What You Gotta Do" has been covered by such a diverse array of singers as Bobby Vee, Johnny Rivers, Al Wilson, Clarence Carter, Tom Jones, Cher and Greg Allman, Jefferson, Nina Simone, The Four Tops, Linda Ronstadt, Sammy Davis Jr., Roberta Flack, Greg Kihn and of course, Webb himself.

"London's Not Too Far" (Marvin being a founder of the original UK Shadows). John Sebastian's "Younger Generation" and Three Dog Night's "One" are two of the better tracks.

1972—Nothin' Like A Sunny Day (Robert Thomas Velline) (United Artists U/A UAS 5656): Every Opportunity • Captain On The Line • Halfway Down The Road • Hayes • My God And I • Going Nowhere • Home • Take Good Care Of My Baby (new version) • Here She Comes Again • It's All The Same

Commentary: A bearded Robert Thomas Velline graces the cover. There is no mention of Bobby Vee. All but two songs are original Robert Velline compositions. A slowed downed, wistful version of Bobby's top hit, "Take Good Care Of My Baby" also appears on the album.

Additional mentions:

1995—Bobby Vee and the Shadows: The Early Rockin' Years (CEMA Special Products S21-18277): Flyin' High • Suzie Baby • Lonely Love • Love Must Have Passed Me By • It's Too late • Laurie • Remember the Day • That'll Be the Day • Susie Q • Butterfly • Party Doll • Bye Bye Love • Wishing • Leave Me Alone (Vocal by Bill Velline) • What'll I Do (Vocal by Bill Velline) • Toy Soldier • Loco • Card Shark • Mindreader

Commentary: Several very good vocals by a very young Bobby Vee and many excellent instrumentals with Bill Velline's stellar guitar work leading the way. It's unique in that brother Bill Velline provides two lead vocals—the only vocals he ever recorded.

1998—Essentials & Collectable Bobby Vee (EMI 7243): Suzie Baby • Devil or Angel • Mr Blue • Rubber Ball • More Than I Can Say • Rockin' Robin • Now There's Only Me • How Many Tears •

Take Good Care of My Baby • Run To Him • All You Got To Do
Is Touch Me • The Idol • Please Don't Ask About Barbara • That's
the Way I'll Come To You • My Golden Chance • Sharing You • It
Might As Well Rain Until September • The Opposite • It Couldn't
Happen To A Nicer Guy • A Forever Kind of Love • Don't Ever
Take Her For Granted • Punish Her • The Night Has A Thousand
Eyes • One Boy too Late • Don't Breathe A Word • On the Street
Where We Grew Up • His Shadow • This Is Your Day • Bobby
Tomorrow • Three On A Date • A Letter From Betty • Be True To
Yourself • Willingly • Never Love A Robin • Hickory, Dick and
Doc • How To Make A Farewell • Where Is She • Every Little Bit
Hurts • Cross My Heart • Keep On Trying • Run Like The Devil •
Butterfly • Come Back When You Grow Up • Beautiful People •
Maybe Just Today • My Girl/Hey Girl • Let's Call It A Day Girl •
No Obligations • So Much Love • Well All Right

Commentary: An excellent collection of hits, obscure album
tracks and rare and unissued tracks. 50 songs in total! Some of the
best of the unreleased tracks are "Three On a Date", "All You
Gotta Do Is Touch Me", "That's the Way I'll Come to You", and
"One Boy Too Late". The final track on Disc One, "Don't Breathe
a Word" is a cover of a Sonny Curtis (Crickets) composition.
Carole King's "It Might As Well Rain Until September", "It
Couldn't Happen To A Nicer Guy", and "My Golden Chance" are
wonderful album track selections. This is a very good, and very
generous sampler from the Bobby Vee Liberty catalog.

**2000—Down the Line (A Buddy Holly Tribute) [40th
Anniversary Edition] Roller Coaster Records (RCCD 3046)
(U.K.):** Down the Line • Rock Me My Baby • Rave On • Midnight
Shift • Look At Me • Tell Me How • Love's Made a Fool of You •
It Doesn't Matter Anymore • I'm Gonna Love You Too • Blue
Days, Black Nights • Love Is Strange • Changin' All Those
Changes • What To Do/Crying, Waiting, Hoping/Learning the

Game • (You're So Square) Baby I Don't Care • Fool's Paradise • Maybe Baby • Holly Hop • Words of Love/Listen To Me

Commentary: Rockhouse also released this in 1999 (RS-5999-1), although it appears with fewer tracks. It's another Holly tribute with several songs Bobby had not previously recorded. This is a good companion piece for his 1962 Crickets collaboration and 1963 Holly tribute LP. Several tunes are done up similar to the Buddy Holly originals, however, many other songs are given pleasant new arrangements.[81]

2003—I Wouldn't Change a Thing (Rockhouse) (Import CD):
Whatever Happened to Peggy Sue • How To Make A Farewell • That's the Way Love Goes • One Way Or Another • Just Today • Cry Myself to Sleep • Right Where You Left Me • Take Good Care of My Baby • Think About That • Wink of An Eye • Story Book Ending • The Night Has A Thousand Eyes • I Wouldn't Change a Thing

Commentary: Listed as a CD import, the disk includes a few old hits (however, done up differently from the original productions), but mostly it contains new Vee tracks. Especially interesting are two Del Shannon covers, "That's the Way Love Goes" and "Cry Myself To Sleep"—neither song of which is considered among Del's many memorable hits. Before Del Shannon's untimely death in 1990, he and Bobby became close friends and Bobby recognizes their friendship with the two songs. The latter song is given a "Come On Little Angel" (The Belmonts) chorus treatment. He also gives "(Maybe) Just Today" another go—a song of which he said he didn't get right the first time. Also of immense interest are two Bobby Vee originals: "I Wouldn't Change a Thing" and "Whatever Happened to Peggy Sue" (written by celebrated British

---

[81] Holly often tinkered with other people's songs—compare his fast AND slow versions of "Slippin' and Slidin'." Both are excellent covers of the Little Richard original, but sound like completely different songs. It's reasonable to conclude that Bobby also tinkered with some of the original arrangements.

lyricist Tim Rice). This CD is the first appearance of Bobby's iconic semi biographical "I Wouldn't Change a Thing", a song that easily could have, and should have been a hit at any time during his career.

2003--Bobby Vee Up North December with Family & Friends (Rockhouse—RH5065): Christmas Lullaby - Prelude • Home For The Holidays • Peace On Earth • Up North December • Electric Trains And You • Little Drummer Boy • White Christmas • Small Town America • (Merry Christmas) Love To You This Year • (Very Merry Holly Jolly) Christmas Holiday • Good King Wenceslas (instrumental) • Christmas Lullaby

Commentary: A Christmas offering from the Vee's own Rockhouse operation with mostly new recordings (but not all). "Electric Trains and You" should be on everyone's holiday song list. "Up North December" is a pleasant mid-tempo number with a Ventures' sounding bass throughout and "Small Town America" provides a melancholy setting for everyone who grew up in a small town. "Christmas Lullaby" is a lovely instrumental.

2004—Merry Christmas From Bobby Vee/The Wonderful World of Bobby Vee (two LP set from BGO—Beat Goes On): Jingle Bell Rock • My Christmas Love • White Christmas • Christmas Vacation • I'll Be Home For Christmas • A Christmas Wish • A Not So Merry Christmas • Silver Bells • Winter Wonderland • Blue Christmas • Silent Night • (There's No Place Like) Home For the Holidays • Charms • A Letter From Betty • All You Gotta Do is Touch Me • On the Street Where We Grew Up • Don't Worry Mary Ann • Be True To Yourself • I Keep Remembering Things I Should Forget • This Is Your Day • Bobby Tomorrow • A Girl I Used To Know • His Shadow • Anyone Else

Commentary: The first album is basically the original *Merry Christmas From Bobby Vee* LP that was issued in 1962, plus the additional "Christmas Vacation". The second LP, *The Wonderful World of Bobby Vee* was not released in '63 as planned. It was finally released in England on compact disc in 2002. "Charms" and "Be True To Yourself" are two of the outstanding tracks. Oddly, except for the artist's photo, the album cover is practically identical to Liberty's *The Wonderful World of Gene McDaniels* and *The Wonderful World of Julie London,* both of which were also released in '63. It appears that Liberty had planned a series of *Wonderful World of...* releases (the label also released *The Wonderful World of Walter Brennan.* Bobby's LP was to be the 4th in the series). That being so, why did the company scrap the Bobby Vee LP? Bobby's cancelled LP included hit song tracks to help drive sales, whereas the other *Wonderful World of...* LPs did not. Perplexing, to say the least.

2005—Last Of The Great Rhythm Guitar Players (PEG) (UK Compact Disc): The Thing About Real Love • It's Your Life • I Wouldn't Change A Thing • Clutches Of Love • Kansas City... Do Wa Do • Hey Friend • What She Sees In Him • Never Felt Quite Like This • Some Kind Of Special Love • Don't Let Your Dreams Go • Take Good Care Of My Baby • The Night Has 1,000 Eyes

Commentary: Backed by his sons on this stellar CD, Bobby turns in one of his best performances! Give a particularly close listen to track 5, "Kansas City... Do Wa Do". It's the most bluesy Bobby has ever been and it makes me wonder what an entire blues album might have sounded like. Would he have reinvented himself the way Dion did when Dion released his highly acclaimed *Bronx in Blue* blues CD? It's certainly possible. Bobby writes all songs on this CD except for the last two, which are his slowed down versions of two of his biggest hits. This is one of those rare discs that a person can arbitrarily select any track and come up with a winner. It compares with the best of the Vee catalog.

2011—Bobby Vee Rarities (EMI Int'l) [2011] (UK Compact Disc): Suzie Baby • Love Must Have Passed Me By • Laurie • White Silver Sands • Foolish Tears • All Cried Out • Make Me Belong To You • Only One Love • You Belong To Me • I'd Sigh I'd Cry • Rockin' Robin • Heartache Of Yesterday • Stagger Lee (feat. The Crickets) • Party Doll (feat. The Crickets) • Just One More Time • Don't Ever Take Her For Granted • Have Yourself A Cry • The Idol • You Won't Forget Me • Tears Wash Her Away • Write Me A Letter Donna • That's The Way I'll Come To You • Johnny & Joanne • I Wish You Were Mine Again • Stranger In Your Arms • Mr. Moonlight • I Don't Want To See You Anymore • Willingly • Hickory, Dick And Doc • Happy With Him • Laugh Of The Year • Not Like It Was With You • Where Is She • Pretend You Don't See Her • Don't Tell Me You Love Me • How To Make A Farewell • Everyday I Have To Cry Some • Let The Four Winds Blow • Weekend • Like Someone In Love • Take A Look Around Me • The Story Of My Life • No One Can Make My Sunshine Smile • You're Thinking Of Him Again • Rhythm Of Love • You'll Be Needing Me Baby • Bittersweet • Gone • Answer Me • Save A Love • It Doesn't Matter • No • Just Like Lookin' In A Mirror • I Can't Hear You • I'm Gonna Make It Up To You • Take Away • Ferguson Road • Dance To The Music • Love In My Love Song • Take Good Care Of My Baby • I Wouldn't Change A Thing.

Commentary: Sixty-one rare, often previously unreleased/unheard Bobby Vee songs for less than ten bucks! A remake of Bobby's first record, "Suzie Baby" starts off the disk, but it's not the song as you remember it. It eases into a slow, orchestrated intro and if you don't have the liner notes handy, you're not sure what song is coming up. About halfway in the beat picks up and Bobby breaks into the familiar refrain "Suzie Baby, Where are you…"[82] It's a splendid surprise and one of the highlights of the entire disk. Also of special note is "Tears Wash Her Away". It's sort of an up-

---

[82] Partial lyrics to Suzie Baby, written by Bobby Vee, Saima Music.

tempo "Run To Him", recorded in 1963, but not available until 2010. The CD ends with the indescribably exquisite "I Wouldn't Change A Thing". These songs, previously unreleased and alternate takes, were masterfully mixed and mastered by Bobby's sons, Jeff and Tommy. The disk also presents many other hard to find songs. It's a must have CD for Bobby Vee fans.

2014—Bobby Vee The Adobe Sessions (Rockhouse) [2014] (Compact Disc): Tuscon Girl • Walls • Old Love Letters • I'm Just A Country Boy • The Man In Me • Save The Last Dance For Me • I Like It That Way • In My Baby's Eyes • I Gotta Know • Never Be Anyone Else But You • If I Needed You • Since I Met You Baby • Window Shopping / Half as Much • Fix It Up • Father to His Son • The Maker • Love Must Have Passed Me By • I'm Gonna Sit Right Down and Write Myself a Letter

Commentary: Diagnosed with Alzheimer's disease, this is most likely Bobby Vee's final CD. It has a raw, downhome feel to it, made up of old favorites and new material. The biggest surprise for me is Bobby's reworking of "In My Baby's Eyes". The original is one of his finest uptempo numbers and it was totally overlooked by his fans. Perhaps this was Bobby saying "if you missed it the first time around, here it is again…" This CD is released on Vee's own Rockhouse Productions label.

***

During the mid 60s, several Bobby Vee albums were released on the Sunset label, a budget album subsidiary that reissued Liberty, Imperial and Minit material. Over the years it offered LPs on Johnny Rivers, Jan and Dean, Fat's Domino, Timi Yuro, Ricky Nelson, The Chipmunks, The Ventures, Don McLean, Gordon Lightfoot, Jay and the Americans, Johnny Burnette, Bobby Goldsboro, Bobby Vee and countless others. Sunset offered a most extensive library of quality low-priced music albums. Specifically regarding the many Bobby Vee Sunset releases, most, if not all, tracks were previously released on Liberty.

***

In 2008, Bobby rerecorded half a dozen of his hits for the K-Tel label, titled *Bobby Vee His Very Best*. The songs are not the original recordings. For most people, seeking out original recordings would be the most satisfactory solution to obtaining Bobby's material. However, true Vee aficionados should not discount the K-Tel offering. The songs may not be the original recordings, but the Vee voice is. There are many who would welcome these "alternate versions".

***

An extensive variety of Bobby's greatest hits, reissues, double LPs, etc, exist and are often readily available via recorded music marketplaces.

11

SINGLES

After his first single in 1959, Liberty Records averaged about four single releases each year for Bobby until 1970 when Liberty merged with United Artists. UA would release three singles over the next few years and then Bobby's contract expired. A couple of independent companies released a few more records, but by 1979 there would be no more singles. This chapter lists each 45-rpm single, including extended play 45s, the label and number, its year of release, and chart position (if applicable).

Bobby Vee's USA 45rpm Discography

1959	Suzie Baby / Flyin' High	Soma 1110
	Suzie Baby (77) / Flyin' High	Liberty 55208
1960	What Do You Want (93) / My Love Loves Me	Liberty 55234
	One Last Kiss (112) / Laurie	Liberty 55251
	Devil or Angel (6) / Since I Met You Baby (81)	Liberty 55270
	Rubber Ball (6) / Everyday	Liberty 55287
1961	Stayin' In (33) / More Than I Can Say (61)	Liberty 55296
	How Many Tears (63) / Baby Face (119)	Liberty 55325
	Take Good Care of My Baby (1) / Bashful Bob	Liberty 55354
	Run To Him (2) / Walkin' With My Angel (53)	Liberty 55388
1962	Please Don't Ask About Barbara (15) / I Can't Say Goodbye (92)	
		Liberty 55419
	Sharing You (15) / In My Baby's Eyes	Liberty 55451
	Punish Her (20) / Someday (99)	Liberty 55479
	Toy Soldier / Card Shark (listed as The Strangers)	Liberty 55481
	A Forever Kind of Love (13) / Remember Me, Huh (UK)	Liberty 10046
1963	The Night Has a Thousand Eyes (3) / Anonymous Phone Call (110)	
		Liberty 55521
	Charms (13) / Bobby Tomorrow	Liberty 55530
	Be True To Yourself (34) / A Letter From Betty (85)	Liberty 55581
	Never Love A Robin (99) / Yesterday and You (55)	Liberty 55636
1964	Stranger In Your Arms (83) / 1963	Liberty 55654
	I'll Make You Mine (52) / She's Sorry	Liberty 55670
	Hickory, Dick or Doc (52) / I Wish You Were Mine Again	Liberty 55700

The Music of Bobby Vee

	Where Is She (120) / How To Make A Farewell	Liberty 55726
1965	Every Little Bit Hurts (84)/Pretend You Don't See Her (97)	Liberty 55751
	Cross My Heart (99) / This Is the End	Liberty 55761
	Keep On Trying (85) / You Won't Forget Me	Liberty 55790
	Run Like The Devil (124) / Take A Look Around Me	Liberty 55828
	Story Of My Life / High Coin	Liberty 55843
1966	A Girl I Used To Know (133) / Gone	Liberty 55854
	Butterfly/Save A Love	*Liberty 55877
	Look At Me Girl (52) / Save A Love	*Liberty 55877
1967	Come Back When You Grow Up (3) / That's All In the Past	**Liberty 55964
	Come Back When You Grow Up (3)/Swahili Serenade	**Liberty 55964
	Beautiful People (37) / I May Be Gone	Liberty 56009
1968	Maybe Just Today (46) / You're A Big Girl Now	Liberty 56014
	My Girl/Hey Girl Medley (35) / Just Keep It Up	Liberty 56033
	Do What You Gotta Do (83) / Thank You	Liberty 56057
	(I'm Into Lookin' For) Someone To Love Me (98) / Thank You	Liberty 56080
1969	Jenny Came To Me / Santa Cruz	Liberty 56096
	Let's Call It A Day Girl (92) / I'm Gonna Make It Up To You	Liberty 56124
1970	In And Out Of Love (111)/Electric Trains and You	Liberty 56149
	No Obligations / Woman In My Life	Liberty 56178
	Sweet Sweetheart (88) / Rock and Roll Music and You	Liberty 56208
1971	Signs / Something To Say	United Artists 50755
	Electric Trains and You/Sweet Sweetheart	United Artists 50875
1973	Take Good Care of My Baby / Every Opportunity	United Artists 199
1974	Don't Matter To Me/I'm Doing Time	GSF-6913
1975	(I'm) Lovin' You / Sayin' Goodbye	Shady Brook 45-013
1976	You're Never Gonna Find Some Like Me	Shady Brook 45-026
	It's Good To Be Here /I Needed You	Shady Brook 45-030
1978	Well All Right / Something Has Come Between Us	United Artists 36370
1979	Tremblin' On/Always Be Each Other's Best Friend	Cognito V-006

Note: Some singles were released twice with a different B-side
Some singles were released with a picture sleeve
Some 45rpm records and EPs were issued in both mono and stereo
(..) The number enclosed indicates its highest USA charting
1962's Liberty 55481 is a release by Bobby's band The Strangers

*   Liberty 55877 used for Butterfly/Save A Love and Look At Me Girl/Save A Love
**   Liberty 55964 used for Come Back When You Grow Up/That's All In the Past and Come Back When You Grow Up/Swahili Serenade

Extended Play 45s:

1961   Devil or Angel – **Liberty 1006:** Devil or Angel; One Last Kiss; What Do You Want; My Love Loves Me
1961   Bobby Vee's Hits – **Liberty 1010**: Rubber Ball; More Than I Can Say; Stayin' In; Young Love
1961   Bobby Vee – **Liberty 1013:** Run To Him; Take Good Care of My Baby; Walkin' With My Angel; How Many Tears
1972   Robert Thomas Velline – **United Artists 85:** (interview) for Disc Jockey

Note: Extended Play 45's (EPs) were mini-albums, generally containing 4-6 tracks from an artist's most recent LP. The 4-track EP was more common in the USA, whereas overseas markets often released as many as 6 tracks.   EPs were a far more common marketing ploy in England, Australia/New Zealand and various European markets than in the USA.   Almost all EPs came in an artful hard paper sleeve.

***

In 1988 and 1989, Rhino Records Inc. issued a 60 disc series of 4-song mini compact discs called *Lil' bit of Gold*. The CDs were packaged in three-inch sleeves with an artist photo and noting the four songs on the disc. To play the discs, the 3" CD had to be inserted into a plastic adapter disc that was the size of a normal CD. Some artists had two volumes, but most were limited to one disc. Among others, the artists included The Four Preps, Jan and Dean, The Fleetwoods, The 4 Seasons and The Everly Brothers. The track listing for the Bobby Vee mini CD (Rhino R3 73019) is: "Take Good Care Of My Baby/Run To Him/The Night Has A Thousand Eyes/Come Back When You Grow Up". These novelty mini CDs are rare and collectible.

***

Note: The discography(s) listed in this book are U.S. only. If you would like to see a United Kingdom listing of his singles, access: http://www.45cat.com/artist/bobby-vee/uk

Some of the rare songs from Bobby's UK catalog include: "Love, Love, Love", "At a Time Like This", "True Love Never Runs Smooth" (Gene Pitney cover), and "(I'm) Loving You". A few of these very rare tracks are from Bobby's Sunny Brook recordings.

It's interesting to note the many extended play (EP) 45s in Bobby's UK catalog (at least 13 EPs).

12

MISCELLANEOUS MUSINGS

Bobby Vee recorded many stellar tracks that could have/should have been hits, but were not for one reason or another. Some of the tracks were issued as singles and didn't catch on. Some were B-sides and others were album tracks that were never released as singles. Still others languished in the Liberty vaults, unheard for decades. I believe a collection of any combination of these songs would have made a heck of an album!

The Album(s) That Could Have Been

Early 60s:

"A Forever Kind of Love" (Not released as a single in the USA. #13 UK single)
"Be True To Yourself" (Single release that charted fairly high #34)
"I Can't Say Goodbye" (B-side #92)
"In My Baby's Eyes" (Excellent B-side rocker that did not chart)
"Little Queenie (Crickets' backed album track rocker)
"My Golden Chance" (Album track only)
"Never Love a Robin" (Flip side that charted #99)
"Pretend You Don't See Her" (Mellow B-side #97)
"Remember Me, Huh" (Album track USA. B-side in the UK)
"Run Like the Devil" (Single that didn't make the Top 100)
"Someday" (B-side. One of his best rockers, only reached #99)
"Stranger In Your Arms" (Single that only charted #83)
"Teardrops Fall Like Rain" (Album track only)
"Tears Wash Her Away" (Unreleased)
"When You're In Love" (Album track, Crickets' backed rocker)
"You Won't Forget Me" (B-side that did not chart)

Mid/Late 60s:

"Butterfly" (Released as a single in 1966, but pulled very quickly)
"Can You Love a Poor Boy" (Album track only)
"Do What You Gotta Do" (A-side that only charted at #83)
"High Coin" (B-side)
"How To Make a Farewell" (B-side)
"I Wouldn't Change A Thing" (Not released as a single)
"Let's Call It A Day Girl" (A-side only charted at #92)
"One" (Album track only)
"Story Book Ending" (Album track only)
"Sunrise Highway" (Album track only)
"Tiffany Rings" (Album track only)
"Turn Down Day" (Album track only)
"You'll Be Needing Me Baby" (Unreleased)

The unquestionably high performance quality of Bobby Vee's music could allow for any number of other songs to be substituted for many above: "Anonymous Phone Call;" "This is Where Friendship Ends;" "Who Am I;" "Theme For a Dream;" "Little Flame;" "Electric Trains and You;" practically any of his Buddy Holly covers and countless others.

Songs in Common

Following is a partial list of some of the songs that both Bobby Vee and others have recorded—but certainly not all. I am making no attempt at sorting them all out or listing every possible variation. Many are Bobby's songs that others covered and many are songs that Bobby covered. I simply include this list for curiosity's sake should you wish to sample other versions of songs that Bobby recorded:

A Fool Never Learns: the Crickets, Andy Williams
A Forever Kind of Love: Cliff Richard
Anonymous Phone Call: Frank Ifield
Beautiful People: Kenny O'Dell
Bo Diddley: Bo Diddley, Buddy Holly, Temptations, Ronnie Hawkins, Kenny Rogers
Brown-eyed Handsome Man: Chuck Berry, Buddy Holly, Waylon Jennings, Johnny Cash, Million Dollar Quartet (Presley, Cash, Perkins, Lewis)

Butterfly: Barry and the Tamerlanes
Candy Man: Roy Orbison, Dion
Can't Get Used to Losing You: Andy Williams
Come Back When You Grow Up: Los Freddy's, Leif Garrett, Shadden and the King Lears, Leif Garrett, Johnny Tillotson
Charms: Rob de Nijs and The Lords (Netherlands)
Cry Myself to Sleep: Del Shannon
Dawn: Four Seasons,
Devil or Angel: Clovers, Johnny Crawford, Jesse Winchester, Hollywood Flames
Do What You Gotta Do: Johnny Rivers, Linda Ronstadt, Clarence Carter, Al Wilson, Roberta Flack, Tom Jones
Everyday: Buddy Holly, James Taylor, Tina Robin, Don McLean, John Denver
From Me to You: Beatles, Del Shannon, The Crickets
(The) Girl Can't Help It: Little Richard, Cliff Richard, Animals, Everly Brothers, Bobby Troup, Led Zeppelin
Go Away Little Girl: Steve Lawrence, Donnie Osmond, Marlena Shaw ("Go Away Little Boy"), Happenings, Dion, Del Shannon, Bobby Vinton, Jonny Mathis, Count Basie
How Many Tears: Tami Lynn
I Can't Say Goodbye: Bobby Rydell
I Gotta Know: Cliff Richard, Elvis Presley
It Might As Well Rain Until September: Helen Shapiro, Gary and Dave, Tony Evans and His Orchestra, Susan Cowsill, Sheena Davis Group, Marquis of Kensington
It'll Be Me: Cliff Richard, Jerry Lee Lewis
Let's Call It A Day Girl: Razor's Edge
Little Queenie: Chuck Berry, Rolling Stones, Adam Faith, Kentucky Headhunters, Dave Berry and the Cruisers, Shakin' Stevens, Troggs, Beatles, Flamin' Groovies, Trashmen
London's Not Too Far: Cliff Richard, Hank Marvin
Look At Me Girl: Playboys of Edinburg
Memphis: Chuck Berry, Johnny Rivers, Elvis Presley
Moon River: Andy Williams, Dion, Jerry Butler, Barry Manilow, countless others
More Than I Can Say: Leo Sayer, Crickets, Shadows (UK), Los Babys, Sammy Kershaw
Mountain of Love: Harold Dorman, Johnny Rivers, Ronnie Dove, Charley Pride, Narvel Felts, Brenda Lee

My Girl/Hey Girl: Temptations, Mamas and Papas, American Breed, Isaac Hayes, Righteous Brothers, Otis Redding/Freddie Scott, Michael McDonald, Billy Joel, Donnie Osmond, George Benson, Carole King

Needles and Pins: Jackie DeShannon, Tom Petty/Nicks, Ramones, Searchers, Smokie

The Night Has A Thousand Eyes: Jimmy Justice, Carpenters, Gary Lewis and the Playboys, Angels, Anita Kelsey, Mud

One: Three Dog Night, Harry Nilsson, New Seekers, Chain Saw Kittens, Dokken

Pretend You Don't See Her: Jerry Vale, Don Cornell

Punish Her: Mike Preston

Raining In My Heart: Buddy Holly, Leo Sayer, Anne Murray, Don McLean, Skeeter Davis, Hank Marvin, Connie Francis

Rubber Ball: Marty Wilde, Gary Lewis and the Playboys

Ruby Baby: Dion, Drifters, Donald Fagin, Ronnie Hawkins, Del Shannon, Beach Boys, Bobby Rydell, Mitch Ryder, Miguel Rios, Bobby Darin, Billy "Crash" Craddock

Run To Him: Donny Osmond, Little Eva and Susie Allanson (Retitled as "Run To Her")

Sharing You: Liverpool Express

Since I Met You Baby: Ivory Joe Hunter, Lou Rawls, Tony Orlando, Sonny James, Dean Martin, Freddie Fender, Jerry Lee Lewis, B.B. King

The Story of My Life: Marty Robbins

Summer in the City: Lovin' Spoonful, Del Shannon, Joe Cocker

Summertime Blues: Eddie Cochran, Cliff Richard, Dion Dimucci, The Who, Joan Jett, Alan Jackson, Beachboys, Blue Cheer, Olivia Newton John, Marty Wilde, Johnny Hallyday, Robert Gordon

Sweet Sweetheart: Carole King

Take Good Care of My Baby: Dion, Bobby Vinton, Beatles, Smokie

Teardrops Fall Like Rain: Crickets, The Grasshoppers

That's the Way Love Is: Del Shannon

Theme For A Dream: Cliff Richard

True Love Never Runs Smooth: Gene Pitney, Don and Juan

Yesterday and You/Armen's Theme: Ross Bagdasarian (David Seville), Si Zentner (Instrumental)

You Won't Forget Me: Jackie DeShannon

You'll Be Needing Me Baby: Nino Tempo and April Stevens, The Lettermen

Younger Generation: John Sebastian (Lovin' Spoonful), Jose Feliciano

Walkin' With My Angel: Herman's Hermits, Ventures (Instrumental)

What Do You Want: Adam Faith, Ersel Hickey, Petula Clark
White Silver Sands: Don Rondo, Bill Black, Sonny James, Ventures, Ronnie Dove, Ace Cannon (Instrumental)

In addition to the above songs (and many more that he recorded as album tracks), Bobby recorded a plethora of Buddy Holly songs—in fact, practically every major Holly song. Bobby performed one or two Buddy Holly songs on many of his early albums, plus he released an entire Holly Tribute album and later updated it and added even more tracks for the eventual compact disc.

Songwriter

Many people mistakenly believe Bobby Vee was simply an interpreter of songs written by others. This is hardly true. As a high school sophomore he penned his debut song "Suzie Baby", while in class—patterning it after Buddy Holly's hit, "Peggy Sue". It became a regional hit on the independent Soma Label and convinced major record companies that he had the talent to become a star. Several companies bid for Bobby's services. He signed with Liberty Records, which released his song nationally. It went to #77.

However, after that it's true that very few of Bobby's compositions made it onto vinyl. But why should he or his record company have shunned the writers who were churning out huge hits for him. By his 6th single, producer Snuff Garrett had "discovered" the hit songwriting team of Gerry Goffin and Carole King, recording their song "How Many Tears". Although it was a modest hit, rising only to #63, it was the first of many Goffin/King songs he would record—with many becoming huge hits.

After his debut single, only rarely did a Vee/Velline composition show up. Bobby's simple, but exquisite "Laurie", was awarded the B-side to "One Last Kiss", but that was pretty much it during the early years. A few previously unreleased songs penned by Bobby showed up many years later on his *Rarities* CD, but they'd been kept hidden away in the vault and never made it onto vinyl.

Bobby recorded for several years before self-written songs began to emerge to any degree. The first sign of this was several self-penned songs on his 1964 *New Sounds From England* LP, "I'll Make You Mine", "She's Sorry", etc.

A year later, "High Coin", a brilliant collaboration effort with Van Dyke Parks, was released as a B-side. It was actually the better of two good sides, but neither side received any attention and quickly died without so much as a whimper.

If nothing else, however, these offerings began a modest increase in Bobby's compositions finding their way onto vinyl—primarily as album tracks. Bobby's final Liberty LP, *Nothin' Like a Sunny Day,* with the artist being credited as Robert Thomas Velline, consisted of eight of the ten tracks being Velline compositions. Freed of Liberty's control, Bobby's future CDs showcased more of his writing. 2005's Last of the Great Rhythm Guitar Players CD saw ten of his songs on the twelve-song disc. It is arguably his best album—at least it certainly ranks among his best.

Following is a list of Bobby Vee/Velline composed songs. Although I suspect some later recordings were also written by Bobby, I am unable to verify the writer(s) of some of those songs and therefore will not include them in this list:

"Annie Joined the Band"
"Any Other Girl"
"Back In Town"
"Captain On the Line"
"Clutches of Love"
"Cross My Heart" (with Curtis & Barrett. Different disc says Curtis & Lesslie)
"Don't Let Your Dreams Go"
"Don't You Believe Them"
"Dry Your Eyes"

Robert Reynolds

"Every Opportunity"
"Ginger" (with Lesslie)
"Going Nowhere"
"Halfway Down the Road"
"Hayes"
"Here She Comes Again"
"Hey Friend"
"High Coin" (with Van Dyke Parks)
"Home"
"I Don't Want to See You Anymore"
"I May Be Gone"
"I Wish You Were Mine Again"
"I Wouldn't Change a Thing"
"I'll Make You Mine"
"I'm Gonna Make it Up To You" (with Thomas "Snuffy" Garrett)
"In and Out of Love"
"In the Past"
"It Doesn't Matter"
"It's All the Same"
"It's Your Life"(with Jeff Velline)
"Kansas City…Do Wa Do"
"Laurie"
"Lover's Goodbye" with Leslie
"Mr. Moonlight"
"Never Felt Quite Like This"(with J. Velline)
"One Way Or Another" (with Jeff Vee)
"Right Where You Left Me" (with Wilson Roberts)
"She's Sorry"
"Silent Partner"
"Small Town America"
"Some Kind of Special Love"
"Something Has Come Between Us"
"Something To Say"
"Story Book Ending"
"Suzie Baby"
"Thank You"
"That's All In the Past"
"The Thing About Real Love"
"Think About That" (with Tom Vee)
"This Is the End"

"This Is Where Friendship Ends" (with T. Leslie)
"What She Sees in Him"
"Whatever Happened to Peggy Sue" (with Tim Rice, Robbie, Jeff & Tommy
       Vee)
"Wink of An Eye" (with Robb Vee)
"Write Me A Letter Donna"
"You're a Big Girl Now"

The Goffin/King Relationship

Many fans of Bobby Vee know that the husband and wife team of
Gerry Goffin and Carole King wrote Bobby's only number one hit,
"Take Good Care of My Baby". Some may know the prolific pair
also wrote some of Bobby's other big hits. Bobby recorded more
than two-dozen of their songs as original releases (both singles and
LP tracks) and he recorded cover versions of Goffin/King songs
that were made into hits by others. To show how closely
Goffin/King and Vee were associated, following is a partial list of
the songs they wrote and that Bobby recorded:

"A Forever Kind of Love" co-written by Goffin with Jack Keller
"Don't Ever Take Her For Granted"
"Ferguson Road" written solely by Carole King
"Go Away Little Girl"
"Hey Girl"
"How Many Tears"
"I Can't Hear You"
"I Can't Say Goodbye"
"If She Were My Girl"
"The Idol"
"In My Baby's Eyes"
"It Might As Well Rain Until September"
"Just One More Time"
"My Golden Chance"
"No One Can Make My Sunshine Smile" co-written Goffin and Jack Keller
"Run To Him" co-written by Goffin and Jack Keller
"Sharing You"

"Sweet Sweetheart"
"Take Good Care of My Baby"
"Tears Wash Her Away"
"Walkin' With My Angel"
"Will You Love Me Tomorrow"
"What About Me"

Other songwriters whose names appear frequently with Bobby Vee recordings: Burt Bacharach and Hal David, and Crickets Jerry Allison and Sonny Curtis. Jack Keller's name appears often with various other composers including Gerry Goffin.

Miscellaneous

Bobby Vee's 30 Hits of the 60's, Volumes 1 & 2, cover a total of 60 hits. The songs on his first four albums are practically all covers—almost 50 more songs. Look up any early album track listing and listen to his and the original artist(s) version for comparison, should you desire.

***

In addition to practically the entire Buddy Holly catalog, a person might want to listen to The Crickets' Liberty sides, especially their singles releases—and in particular "I'm Feeling Better". Bobby, who wrote the song, added his vocals to that of Cricket Jerry Allison during that session. Along with their close recording association, The Crickets joined Bobby on a UK tour in November 1962.

***

With Bobby suffering early stages of Alzheimer's, sons Jeff and Tommy began an archiving project last summer converting hundreds of hours of analogue recordings to digital format. There's urgency to the project because much of the material is on tape—cassette, two-track reels and acetate discs—and tape deteriorates over time. It's especially important they accomplish their objective quickly so their dad can hear the old material and it invoke memories they believe may be therapeutic.

Along with myriad projects, the boys were also responsible for mixing and mastering the many tracks on the *Rarities* CD of 2010. They recently discovered an acetate disc from 1964 in which Bobby hosted a half hour radio show. There's belief the disc may contain rare Buddy Holly recordings, but as of this writing no one knows for sure what's on it.

***

Listen to the beautiful "I Wouldn't Change A Thing". Bobby's voice had matured to the point of sounding similar to Neil Diamond—at least at the opening of the song.

From its simple repetitive strummed opening chords to its timeless message of life with no regrets, "I Wouldn't Change A Thing" is a testament to enduring love: "We've had our breakups, we've had our breakdowns. We've danced with our feet off the ground, making beautiful music and beautiful sounds. I wouldn't change a thing…"[83] It's also a tribute to Bobby Vee's incredible storybook career. Written by Bobby, this heartfelt song is as good as anything this legend recorded during his memorable career.

Perhaps the most appropriate title for this book would be *I Wouldn't Change A Thing*, but it's been used as a title for previous Bobby Vee articles and to use it again would be redundant.

***

And finally, an interesting note of trivia. It's proof that no matter how skilled a person is at choosing topnotch songs, you can't always get them right. Perhaps this is the fickleness of selecting a number one.

As previously mentioned, Dion declined to release Goffin/King's "Take Good Care of My Baby", which Bobby recorded for his only number one single. Bobby turned down Goffin/King's "Go Away Little Girl", which became a #1 record for Steve Lawrence AND #1 for Donny Osmond years later.

According to the Internet website *Classicbands.com*, in 1965 Snuff Garrett was producing a new group called Gary Lewis and

---

[83] Partial lyrics to "*I Wouldn't Change A Thing*", R. Velline. Saima Music Company. 2002.

the Playboys. Lewis' famous father, cinema funny man Jerry
Lewis, lived two doors from Garrett. Garrett presented to the
group a song that Bobby Vee had turned down—"This Diamond
Ring". The group's debut recording went to #1 on February 20,
1965.

The Music of Bobby Vee

13

OVERSEAS

At the height of his extremely successful career, Bobby Vee achieved immense popularity overseas, often realizing the pinnacle of chart success with his recordings. Similarly, he participated regularly in successful overseas tours (England, Australia, Japan, Scandinavia, etc). He continued to frequently perform overseas even after he no longer had hit records. These are some of this treasured entertainer's worldwide accomplishments:

Collection of Hits:

United Kingdom: By 1963 Bobby Vee had collected 10 Top 40 hits. His singles appeared on the UK charts for a total of 134 weeks and his *Bobby Vee Meets the Crickets* album rose to #3, remaining on the charts for several months. He and The Crickets followed up the album with a tour of Great Britain. Ten singles placed #29 or better, seven of them in the Top Ten. Seven albums made the Top Twenty, with five of them in the Top Ten.

UK Top Ten Singles:

1961	"Rubber Ball"	# 4	London HLG 9265
1961	"More Than I Can Say"	# 4	London HLG 9316
1961	"How Many Tears"	#10	London HLG 9389
1961	"Take Good Care of My Baby"	# 3	London HLG 9438
1961	"Run To Him"	# 6	London HLG 9470
1962	"Sharing You"	#10	Liberty LIB 55451
1963	"The Night Has A Thousand Eyes"	# 3	Liberty LIB 10069

Three more singles scored in the UK Top Thirty.

UK Top Ten Albums:

1962	*Take Good Care of My Baby*	# 7	London HAG 2428
1962	*Bobby Vee Meets the Crickets*	# 3	LibertyLBY1084*/1086
1963	*Recording Session*	#10	Liberty LBY 1084*
1963	*Golden Greats*	#10	Liberty LBY 1112
1980	*Singles Album*	# 5	UA UAG 30253

Two more albums made the UK Top Twenty.

*A UK Top Ten Albums reference source lists both *Meets the Crickets* and *Recording Session* LPs with the same label number (1084). It's unknown if Liberty Records did in fact assign the same number to both albums or if one of the numbers is a misprint. A second source lists *Meet the Crickets* as #1086, although album release dates show *Meets the Crickets* as being released before *Recording Session*. Also, various sources conflict over the year of release for *Recording Session*—some show it as 1962 while others show 1963. The former seems more logical because that coincides with the mid 1962 release date in the USA.

The following songs in the larger print were released in the UK as singles, although not so in the USA. Some, but not all, were released as album tracks in the USA:

1962	"A Forever Kind of Love/Remember Me, Huh"
1963	"At A Time Like This/Sharing You"
1963	"Tenderly Yours/The Night Has A Thousand Eyes"
1965	"True Love Never Runs Smooth/Hey Little Girl"
1967	"Like You've Never Known Before/Growing Pains"
1967	"Let the Four Winds Blow/Come Back When You Grow Up"
1969	"Sunrise Highway/(I'm Into Looking For) Someone To Love Me"

"At A Time Like This" and "True Love Never Runs Smooth" are UK only releases. The latter can be found on *The Singles Collection* three-disc set. An excellent cover of Gene Pitney's, Bacharach/David composed, 1963 hit.

Australia/New Zealand: Placed 14 songs in Top 40 singles charts, including six in the top five and two number ones in Australia. "More Than I Can Say" and "Take Good Care Of My Baby" were Top Ten in New Zealand.

Australian Top Ten Singles:

1961 "One Last Kiss"	#1	London HL 1744
1961 "Rubber Ball"	#1	London HL 1745
1961 "Baby Face"	#4	London HL 1818
1961 "Take Good Care of My Baby"	#2	London HL 1855
1961 "Run To Him"	#3	London HL 1900
1962 "The Night Has a Thousand Eyes"	#3	Liberty LIB 55521

Seven more singles landed in the Australian Top Thirty.

Other Locales: In little time Bobby Vee became a worldwide sensation, scoring hit records around the globe. For example, Bobby placed four Top Ten singles in Hong Kong, two in Israel, one in The Philippines and one in Chile. France, Portugal, Spain, Norway, Germany, Mexico, South Africa, Holland, Japan...also produced hits for the young man. Fans throughout the world tuned in to hear Bobby Vee. It was a relationship that would endure beyond the release Bobby's final CD and his retirement as a performer.

The Music of Bobby Vee

PART THREE

14

RECOGNITION and ACCOLADES

During his remarkable career, Bobby Vee received numerous awards, honors and tributes:

Six U.S. Gold Record singles:

"Devil or Angel"
"Rubber Ball"
"Take Good Care Of My Baby"
"Run To Him"
"The Night Has a Thousand Eyes"
"Come Back When You Grow up"

Gold Album:

The Bobby Vee Singles Album (UK) (2006)

Halls of Fame recognition:

- 2004 Bobby Vee Inducted into Mid-America Music Hall of Fame
- 2005 Bobby Vee and the Shadows inducted into Mid-America Music HOF
- 2008 Robert Velline Lifetime Achievement Recipient Mid-America HOF
- 2009 Inducted into Hit Parade Hall of Fame
- Inducted into Rockabilly Hall of Fame on March 28, 2011 (Inductee #225)
- Inducted into the Scandinavian-American Hall of Fame in 2014[84]

---

[84] On October 1, 2014, Bobby Vee, Doc Severinson, and Sig Hansen were inducted into the Scandinavian-American Hall of Fame.

- **2004 Bill Velline Lifetime Achievement Recipient Mid-America HOF**

Other recognitions:

- Music industry publication *Billboard Magazine* recognized Bobby Vee as "One of the ten most consistent chart makers ever."[85]

In annual reader's polls by the sixties music magazine *The Beat Goes On*, Bobby Vee was voted:

- **Best American Act in 1991**
- **Best Live Performer in 1992**
- **Favorite Male Singer in 1994**
- **Runner Up to Paul McCartney as "Most Accomplished Performer" in 1994**

- On June 20, 1999 Bobby proudly received a special honor—*The Theodore Roosevelt Rough Rider Award*. The award is North Dakota's highest recognition for native North Dakotans. During the induction ceremony, ND Governor Ed Schafer said, "Throughout his success, Bobby has maintained his North Dakota roots and values. He is praised by many of his peers not only for being a talented performer, but a kind, good and humble person. I am extremely proud to honor him with this award."[86]

Regarding having received the award, Bobby humbly remarked, ``I've had gold records, and I've had some wonderful honors from a business standpoint. But for somebody from your home state to slap you on the back and say, good job, that's a whole different deal."[87]

Severinson, the longtime bandleader for the Johnny Carson Show and Hansen the star and advisor for the Discovery Channel's documentary TV series *Deadliest Catch*.

[85] North Dakota Office of the Governor, Date not available

[86] Excerpt from Bobby Vee Biography. http://www.bobbyvee.com/bio.html

[87] The Free Library, News Lite, June 22, 1999

- Bobby's brief musical association with Bob Dylan is mentioned in Martin Scorsese's 2005 Dylan documentary, *No Direction Home*. Furthermore, during a 2013 concert in St. Paul, MN, Dylan made special recognition of Bobby Vee, saying, "the most meaningful person I've ever been on stage with, was a man who is here tonight, who used to sing a song called "Suzie Baby". I want to say that Bobby Vee is actually here tonight. Maybe you can show your appreciation with just a round of applause. So, we're gonna try to do this song, like I've done it with him before once or twice."

- In May 2008, the United Kingdom released the compact disc *The Very Best of Bobby Vee*. Almost fifty years after his phenomenal run of hits, Bobby Vee's CD went Top Five in Great Britain—an amazing achievement. Three years later EMI/UK released *Rarities*, a double CD with 61 tracks, many previously unreleased, alternate takes, as well as tracks from his *Bobby Vee On Tour* album cleaned of the "canned" audience reactions.

- Considerable Bobby Vee material is released in *Best Of, Greatest Hits*, and *Rarities* formats. There seems no end to the demand for his material.

In the 90's, Bobby released a 17-track collector's edition cassette, *U.K. Tour '90,* with his sons on his Rockhouse Record Label—an anthology of hits, new material and previously unreleased songs.

And in '94, critics gave high praise to Bobby's *Last Of the Great Rhythm Guitar Players* cassette project. Except for the last two tracks, his slowed down reworking of two old hits, the songs are new material and Bobby writes all. By then his career having spanned 35 years, it's perhaps one of his very best offerings. In 2007, Rockhouse issued this exceptional album on compact disc.

In Summary:

Few artists were as dependable with record sales and charted hits during the early 60's era than was Bobby Vee. The results of his work, the abundance of quality recordings and his long-lasting fan appreciation place him within a very small group of popular music hit makers during that era.

Likewise, few at the time were as innovative, as he recorded concept albums (*Bobby Vee Meets the Crickets, Bobby Vee Meets the Ventures, I Remember Buddy Holly*, and his *30's Hits of the 60's, Volumes 1 and 2)* long before the Beach Boys and Beatles recorded their acclaimed *Pet Sounds* and *Sergeant Pepper* LPs, respectively.

From his 1959 charting of "Suzie Baby", his very first nationally released record, to 1970's "Sweet Sweetheart"; Bobby Vee's music was consistently on the record charts. A Top 100 mainstay for eleven consecutive years (1959-70), his charting of 38 singles is an enviable and an incredible achievement for any artist. His single records charted at numbers one, two, three (twice) and six (twice). Almost 50-years after that winter tragedy in Iowa gave Bobby Vee his opportunity, a collection of his music broke into the Top Five in Great Britain.

Unlike many in the entertainment world there are no scandals to mark his career. No involvement with drugs, no alcoholic fits, no vandalized hotel rooms. He remained faithfully wed to the single true love of his life Karen for more than fifty-years, until her recent passing. There are no stories of impudence, disrespect or rudeness. Although his career was larger than life, his soft-spoken, polite character never changed from the well-mannered young man who set the music world on fire during the early sixties.

Robert Thomas Velline, Bobby Vee, is one of the most beloved and successful performers the music industry has ever produced, aptly filling a void when three other rising stars perished. He's given us an incomparable legacy of some of the best pop/rock music of his generation. We can only judge Bobby Vee by his music—and that's how it should be.

On October 24, 2016, Bobby Vee lost his battle against Alzheimer's. His music carries on.

END

The Music of Bobby Vee

Robert Reynolds

Sources:

Album Liner Notes (LP and Compact Disc) in no particular order: Among several, *Bobby Vee Legendary Masters; Bobby Vee and the Shadows: The Early Rockin' Years; Bobby Vee Rarities; I Remember Buddy Holly; Bobby Vee Meets the Crickets; Bobby Vee Meets the Ventures; Merry Christmas from Bobby Vee and Wonderful World of Bobby Vee; Take Good Care of My Baby; Recording Session; The Night Has a Thousand Eyes; New Sound From England; Live, On Tour; Hits of the Rockin' 50's; Strings and Things; Bobby Vee; Sings Your Favorites; Golden Greats; Golden Greats, Vol. 2; 30 Big Hits of the 60's; 30 Big Hits of the 60's, Vol. 2; The Essential and Collectible Bobby Vee; Look at Me Girl/Come Back When You Grow Up; Just Today/Do What You Gotta Do; Gates, Grills and Railings/Nothin' Like a Sunny Day; The Last of the Great Rhythm Guitar Players; I Wouldn't Change a Thing* (Many of the liners notes are credited to Bob Celli). *The Crickets The Liberty Years; The Crickets Ravin' On From California to Clovis; The Crickets File 1961-1965; The Crickets Something Old, Something New, Something Blue, Something Else*

Baenan, Jeff: *Former Pop Idol Bobby Vee Still Has Reasons to Sing.* Twin Cities Pioneer Press. February 2, 2014.

Barry, Mark. *Rhino's "Lil' Bit Of Gold" 3" CD-Singles Series - A List Of All 60 Titles.* (Mark Barry's Discography Internet Website) April 30, 2009.

Billboard Music Week (Online periodical), Various articles and publication dates.

Billboard Music Week's 1963 Who's Who in the World of Music. Billboard Publications.

bobbyvee.com Internet website

Branson.com. *Original Stars At American Bandstand Are Coming to Branson.* Undated.

Bream, Jon. *Take Good Care of My Baby: Bobby Vee and his wife celebrate 50 years.* (Minneapolis) Star Tribune. April 13, 2014.

Bronson, Fred. *The Billboard Book of Number One Hits.* Billboard Publications, 1985.

Cashbox Magazine Music Charts, various dates.

Celli, Bob. Head of Bobby Vee fan and collector's clubs, and noted Bobby Vee historian. Many of the liner notes for LPs and CDs are credited to Mr. Celli.

Civil Aeronautics Board Report, released September 23, 1959.

The Music of Bobby Vee

City of Lubbock/Buddy Holly Center/Buddy Holly Biography Internet website. Uncredited author.

Dimucci, Dion with Davin Seay. *The Wanderer (Dion's Story)*. Beech Tree Books, Morrow. 1988.

Dominic, Serene. *Song By Song: The ultimate Burt Bacharach reference for fans, serious collectors, and music critics.* Schirmer Trade Books. 2003.

Dylan, Bob. Lyrics from *The Times They Are A-Changin'*. Special Rider Music.

Gilbert, Bob and Gary Theroux. *The Top Ten 1956-Present.* Fireside. 1982.

Goldrosen, John. *The Buddy Holly Story.* The Bowling Green University Press. 1975.

Hi-Teen Magazine. Hi-Teen Publications. Vol. 1, No. 3. January 1963.

Huey, Pamela. *Buddy Holly: The tour from hell.* (Minneapolis) Star Tribune, February 3, 2009.

Huey, Pamela. *The Day the Music Died: Buddy Holly.* Deseret News. January 30, 2009.

Internet Movie Database (IMDB) regarding cinematic film appearances.

Internet article entitled Payola: http://www.history-of-rock.com/payola.htm (Author and date not provided).

Internet webpage TSORT, Song Artist 484, Bobby Vee. http://tsort.info/music.shrqep.htm

Ivers, Gail. *Business Central (For Business Leaders of Central Minnesota – St. Cloud Chamber of Commerce).* January/February 2012.

James, Gary. *Interview With Bobby Vee.* Classicbands.com website. No date available.

James, Tommy, with Martin Fitzpatrick. *Me, the Mob, and the Music.* A Scribner book. February 2010.

Lamb, John. *Inforum: Bobby Vee's Music Lives on with help of family and some high-profile fans.* February 2. 2015.

Leigh, Spencer. *Mersey Beat.* http://www.spencerleigh.co.uk/tag/merseybeat/mersey/. May 29, 2013.

Minneapolis/St Paul Air Port, weather history.

Robert Reynolds

http://www.wunderground.com/history/airport/KMSP/1959/1/31/DailyHistory.html?req_city=&req_state=&req_statename=&reqdb.zip=&reqdb.magic=&reqdb.wmo=

Moore, Craig. *I Wouldn't' Change a Thing.* Goldmine Magazine.(Six installments) April 30-May 19, 2009.

Music Outfitters Internet website. *Bobby Vee.* Uncredited author. Date not available.

Musso, Anthony P. *Setting the Record Straight, Volume 2.* Author House. 2009

Pioneer Public TV.*Postcards: Bobby Vee and the Shadows: Family and Friends.*Web interview. May 14, 2012.

Pop Archives: http://www.poparchives.com.au/161/judy-stone/born-a-woman

Rare Rockin' Records website: *Bob Celli Talks About Upcoming Bobby Vee Release.* December 29, 2010.

Read, Mike; Nigel Goodall and Peter Lewry. *The Complete Chronicle – Cliff Richard.* Hamlyn. 1993.

Record World (also known as *Record Vendor* pre-1964) *Magazine.*

Rockhouse Productions Internet website. rockhousepro.com.

Rolling Stone Encyclopedia of Rock & Roll. A Rolling Stone Press Book/Summit Books. Edited by Jon Pareles and Patricia Romanowski. 1983.

Rolontz, Bob. *Liberty Ties Victor For Singles Lead (Mercury, Decca 45 Runners Up) Billboard Music Week.* June 30, 1962.

Shannon, Bob and John Javna. *Behind the Hits.* Warner Books, Inc. 1986.
Sons Preserve Bobby Vee's Recordings. Uncredited author. St. Cloud Times, MN. February 3, 2015.

Sklar, Ronald. *Bobby Vee.* PopEntertainment. 1999.

Tarbox, James M. *The Day Buddy Holly Died: Bobby Vee Remembers.* Knight-Ridder Newspapers. March 29, 1985.

Teen Pin-ups Magazine. Em Tee Publications. Vol. 2, No. 1. January 1963.

Various Internet Sources

Various Wikipedia sources.

The Music of Bobby Vee

*Wall Street Journal. Singer Dion Dimucci on How a Family Fight Saved His Life.*Uncredited. Aug 26, 2015.

The Washington Times.   Three New Inductees to Scandinavian-American Hall. Associated Press (no author credit available). August 21, 2014.

Thank you for reading *The Music of Bobby Vee*. I hope you found it entertaining and informative. Similar books about other singers and musicians are planned.

Other books by Robert Reynolds are available at major bookstores and online booksellers such as Amazon, Barnes&Noble, Gohastings, Books-a-million, etc and from the following publishers:

AmericanStar:
http://www.americastarbooks.net/sc/productsearch.cgi?storeid=*1a5ce440a0a34abc0842724ed84a15&search_field=robert+reynolds

Firing at Shadows
A Perilous Place
Settler
East of Nowhere
Sentinels in the Sun
Monkeys in the Sun

Black Rose Writing:
http://www.blackrosewriting.com/search?q=robert%20reynolds

Thunder Bay
Sorrowful

Lulu Publishing:
https://www.lulu.com/shop/search.ep?keyWords=robert+reynolds&type=

Trouble's Garden

The Music of Bobby Vee

Along the Quay
Showers In the Rain
A Fine Gray Rain
The Music of Hamilton, Joe Frank
& Reynolds
The Music of Johnny Rivers
Gray Wolf Pass (coming soon)

All books are available in print. Many are available electronically including PDF (many at buyer discount).

Robert   Reynolds   can   be   contacted   via   email   at bobandhoang@yahoo.com

Printed in Great Britain
by Amazon

43583543R00085